CLYDE RIVER-STEAMERS
1872 – 1922

"Columba"

Photo. by Messrs. Maclure, Macdonald & Co. Glasgow

CLYDE RIVER-STEAMERS
1872 – 1922

BY
ANDREW M'QUEEN

WITH FORTY-EIGHT ILLUSTRATIONS

THE STRONG OAK PRESS

This edition © Spa Books & The Strong Oak Press 1990

All rights reserved. No part of this publication may be reproduced, stored in a retrieval system or transmitted in any form, by any means electrical or mechanical or otherwise without first seeking the written permission of the copyright owner and of the publisher.

ISBN: 1-871048-17-6

Publishing History: This work was first issued in 1923 when the title was *CLYDE RIVER STEAMERS Of The Last Fifty Years*. For the sake of clarity the title has been altered so that the fifty years in question are precisely defined. The text and illustrations are reproduced here complete and unabridged.

Published by The Strong Oak Press
          Spa Books Ltd
          PO Box 47
          Stevenage
          Herts SG2 8UH

Printed in Great Britain by Bookcraft (Bath) Ltd.

PREFACE

A LECTURE, entitled "Clyde Steamers of Four Decades," written some ten years ago and delivered at various centres in Glasgow, Lanarkshire and Renfrewshire, forms the basis of this book.

The appreciation invariably displayed by my audiences, and the wish, repeatedly expressed by them, that the matter were accessible in print have encouraged me to amplify my remarks to an extent impossible within the limits of a lecture, and publish them in book form.

The present volume, dealing as it does only with the period lying within my own memory, and compiled mainly from personal recollection, is in no sense intended as a rival to Captain Williamson's delightful history of "The Clyde Passenger Steamer," published nearly twenty years ago. I feel confident, however, that it will appeal to that large circle who take an interest in the Clyde river-fleet, and more particularly, perhaps, to my own contemporaries, who, having also reached the "fogey" stage, are inclined, like myself, towards the rôle of "laudator temporis acti."

To such, the illustrations, all photographic, will recall many an old-time "crack," long since departed.

I have to express my thanks to those photographers, professional and amateur, who have given me permission to reproduce their pictures, and also to all friends who have contributed information regarding any of the boats.

ANDREW M'QUEEN

SHAWLANDS
December 1922

CONTENTS

PART I
THE FLEET, HALF A CENTURY AGO

CHAPTER I

	PAGE
INTRODUCTORY	3

"Industry"

CHAPTER II

HUTCHESON'S VETERANS	9

"Inveraray Castle"—"Mary Jane"—"Iona" No. 3—"Mountaineer" No. 1—"Chevalier"

CHAPTER III

SAILINGS FROM THE BROOMIELAW . . .	17

"Guinevere" — "Vale of Clwyd" — "Bonnie Doon" No. 1—"Gael"—"Kintyre"—"Sultan"—"Sultana" — "Vivid" — "Vesta" — "Carrick Castle"

CHAPTER IV

MORE SAILINGS FROM THE BROOMIELAW . .	27

"Eagle" — "Rothesay Castle" — "Lorne" — "Undine"— "Elaine" — "Vulcan" — "Marquis of Bute"—"Athole"—"Ardencaple," "Ardgowan" and "Levan"—"Craigrownie"—"Lancelot"

CHAPTER V

RAILWAY STEAMERS 37

"Argyle" — "Venus" — "Largs" — "Lady Gertrude"—"Dandie Dinmont" No. 1—"Gareloch"—"Chancellor" No. 2—"The Lady Mary"—"Heather Bell"

CHAPTER VI

VARIOUS BOATS 45

"Hero"—"Marquis of Lorne"—"Balmoral"—"Dunoon Castle"—"Petrel"—"Kingstown"

PART II
ADDITIONS DURING THE PERIOD

CHAPTER VII

THE FIRST FIVE YEARS 59

"Windsor Castle"—"Viceroy"—"Bonnie Doon" No. 2—"Benmore"—"Prince of Wales"—"Sheila" "Adela"—"Glen Rosa" No. 1—"Lord of the Isles" No. 1—"Lough Foyle"

CHAPTER VIII

FROM THE "COLUMBA" TO THE OPENING OF THE GOUROCK ROUTE 75

"Columba"—"Brodick Castle"—"Kinloch"—"Edinburgh Castle" — "Ivanhoe" — "Scotia"—"Chancellor" No. 3—"Minard Castle"—"Meg Merrilies"—"Jeanie Deans"—The "Cluthas"—"Diana Vernon" — "Davaar" — "Grenadier" — "Waverley" No. 2—"Madge Wildfire"—"Victoria" "Seagull" — "Lucy Ashton" — "Fusilier"

CONTENTS

CHAPTER IX

FROM THE OPENING OF THE GOUROCK ROUTE TO THE COMING OF THE TURBINE 89

"Caledonia" — "Galatea" — "Marchioness of Breadalbane" and "Marchioness of Bute" — "Duchess of Hamilton" — "Argyll" — "Cygnus" "Marchioness of Lorne" — "Lady Clare" and "Lady Rowena" — "Lord of the Isles" No. 2 — "Herald" — "Neptune" and "Mercury" — "Glen Sannox" — "Isle of Arran" — "Minerva" and "Glen Rosa" No. 2 — "Culzean Castle" — "Duchess of Rothesay" — "Redgauntlet" — "Dandie Dinmont" No. 2 — "Glenmore" — "Jupiter" — "Talisman" — "Strathmore" — "Kylemore" — "Juno" — "Kenilworth" — "Waverley" No. 3.

CHAPTER X

THE PRESENT CENTURY 107

"King Edward" — "Queen Alexandra" No. 1 — "Mars" — "Duchess of Montrose" — "Duchess of Fife" — "Cygnet" — "Duchess of Argyll" — "Atalanta" — "Marmion" — "Eagle III." — "Mountaineer" No. 3 — "Queen Alexandra" No. 2 — "Queen Empress" — "Fair Maid"

CHAPTER XI

GENERAL REMARKS 119

APPENDIX I

THE "CLUTHAS" 129

APPENDIX II

LIST OF PASSENGER STEAMERS IN THE CLYDE FIRTH TRADE SINCE 1872 132

LIST OF ILLUSTRATIONS

1. "COLUMBA"	. . . .	*Frontispiece*
		PAGE
2. "INVERARAY CASTLE"	. . . .	9
3. "GLENCOE," EX-"MARY JANE"	. . .	12
4. "IONA" NO. 3	. . . . . .	13
5. THE BROOMIELAW IN THE SEVENTIES	. .	17
6. "GAEL"	. . . .	20
7. "SULTANA"	. . . .	22
8. THE BROOMIELAW ABOUT 1885	. . .	27
9. "EAGLE" AT THE BROOMIELAW ABOUT 1865	.	29
10. "ELAINE"	. . . .	30
11. "MARQUIS OF BUTE" AT THE BROOMIELAW	.	31
12. "ATHOLE"	. . . .	34
13. WEMYSS BAY PIER AND FLEET ABOUT 1875	.	37
14. "LADY GERTRUDE"	. . . . .	39
15. "DANIEL ADAMSON," EX-"SHANDON"	. .	42
16. "BALMORAL"	. . . . . .	47
17. "ARRAN," EX-"DUNOON CASTLE"	. . .	50
18. THE BROOMIELAW ABOUT 1876	. . .	59
19. "VICEROY"	. . . .	60
20. "BENMORE" LEAVING THE BROOMIELAW	.	61
21. "BENMORE" AS SHE APPEARED IN 1887	.	63
22. "GUY MANNERING," EX-"SHEILA"	. .	67
23. "LORD OF THE ISLES" NO. 1	. . .	72
24. "BRODICK CASTLE"	. . . . .	76

		PAGE
25. "EDINBURGH CASTLE"	. . . .	77
26. "IVANHOE"	. . . . .	78
27. "JEANIE DEANS" LEAVING ROTHESAY	. .	83
28. "VICTORIA"	. . . . .	86
29. "LUCY ASHTON"	. . . .	87
30. "GALATEA"	. . . . . .	90
31. "DUCHESS OF HAMILTON"	. . .	91
32. "LORD OF THE ISLES" NO. 2	. . .	94
33. "MERCURY"	. . . . .	96
34. "GLEN SANNOX"	. . . .	97
35. "ISLE OF ARRAN"	. . . .	98
36. "CULZEAN CASTLE"	. . . .	99
37. "DUCHESS OF ROTHESAY"	. . .	100
38. "DANDIE DINMONT" NO. 2	. . .	101
39. "JUPITER"	. . . . . .	102
40. "WAVERLEY" NO. 3	. . . .	104
41. "KING EDWARD"	. . . . .	107
42. "QUEEN ALEXANDRA" NO. 1	. . .	108
43. "DUCHESS OF ARGYLL"	. . . .	111
44. "ATALANTA"	. . . . .	112
45. "EAGLE III."	. . . . .	113
46. "QUEEN ALEXANDRA" NO. 2	. . .	114
47. "QUEEN EMPRESS"	. . . .	115
48. "CLUTHA NO. 6"	. . . . .	129

PART I
THE FLEET, HALF A CENTURY AGO

CHAPTER I

INTRODUCTORY

OF the hundred and ten years or so that have passed since the waters of the Clyde were first navigated by a steam vessel, some fifty lie within the compass of my recollection, and I propose, in the following pages, to give some account of the steamers which maintained the passenger traffic on our river and firth in the early seventies, together with the many others that have come and gone since that rather remote time.

Fifty years ago the Clyde fleet consisted for the most part of comparatively new boats, and was in this respect a marked contrast to the fleet of to-day. The majority of the steamers then running had been launched since 1864. This state of affairs was due largely to the American Civil War in 1861-62 and '63, and the demand it had created for fast steamers to run the blockade which the Federals had established outside the Confederate ports of Charleston and Wilmington. Nassau, in the Bahamas, some six or seven hundred miles distant, was the head-quarters of the traffic, a traffic so lucrative, although attended with big risks, that a couple of successful trips were usually sufficient to clear the whole cost of the vessel and leave a profit. For successful blockade-running, the boats had to be fast, handy and of light draught : fast, to run away when pursued; handy, to steer through narrow and tortuous channels; and shallow, to pass in safety over shoals and sandbanks, where the deeper and comparatively clumsy vessels of the blockading fleet dared not follow. The Clyde river-steamers of that time, none of which drew more than five feet of water, whose proportion of length to beam rendered them sensitive to the helm, and whose average speed was probably higher than that of any other class of vessel then afloat, were promptly fixed upon as ideal craft for the enterprise; they were eagerly sought after, prices far too tempting for their owners to refuse were offered and freely paid, with the result that the Clyde was practically denuded of its best boats. In the newspapers of the time we find frequent references to the inroads that were being made on the fleet. The *Herald* of 11th May 1863 had a leader lamenting the departure of the " Ruby," " Neptune," " Pearl," " Kelpie," " Eagle," " Juno," " Jupiter," " Vesta " and " Mail." Two days later it was intimated that the " Spunkie " had been sold to run the blockade. On the 18th it was reported that the steamer " Gem," plying in the Glasgow and Rothesay trade, " was last week sold to the Eastern potentate who has made such havoc of late amongst our crack steamers." (The Eastern potentate, referred to elsewhere as the Emperor of China, was, of course, merely a name put forward as a disguise to conceal the real purchaser.) On 15th June following we are told that the " unknown potentate " has turned his attention to the swift steamer " Rothesay Castle," but that no treaty has yet been concluded. Eleven days later the sale of this vessel for £8500 was chronicled. On the 11th of November in the same year we read that Messrs Hutcheson & Co.'s magnificent saloon steamer " Iona " had been sold for £20,000, and that her handsome deck saloon had been removed and other preparations made for a voyage across the Atlantic.

An insight into the interesting and exhilarating work that awaited such of the boats as survived the passage out can be obtained from Mr William Watson's delightful " Adventures of a Blockade-runner," in which he describes a trip which he made from Galveston to Tampico towards the close of the war, in command of the " Jeanette," formerly the Glasgow and Rothesay passenger steamer " Eagle." He tells how, after escaping from a Yankee cruiser which had put a shot through his funnel, he found that the weight of cotton bales, piled round the boiler as a protection, was causing the steamer to sag amidships, and threatening to break her back. The bales were removed in a hurry, and distributed more evenly over the ship, bow and stern sank to their normal positions, and Tampico was reached in safety.

None of the blockade-runners, so far as I can trace, re-crossed the Atlantic, although some of them survived for many years in American waters, and one, the " Star," is still afloat at Nassau.

The few boats left on the Firth were mostly such as had been esteemed too old or too slow to engage successfully in blockade-running, yet the owners of these had little reason to regret that they had not sold them, for in the absence of their swifter sisters, they reaped a rich harvest in their native waters until such time as a new fleet could be built. It was this new fleet, with the addition of a few of the older vessels alluded to, that maintained the service when my recollections begin in 1872.

There were few sensational performers among the new boats, and no attempt was made to revive the great speed contests of the early sixties, when " Ruby," " Rothesay Castle " and " Neptune " raced one another " hell for leather " all the way from the Broomielaw to Gourock, to the great delight of their passengers, the fining of their skippers, and the glory of their owner-builders, Henderson of Renfrew, Simons of Renfrew and Napier of Govan. Those were the days when Captain Dicky Price, anxious to prevent a rival steamer from getting too far ahead, started the " Ruby " from Dunoon pier while the passengers were embarking, and steamed off, leaving the gangway with passengers on it, sticking over the edge of the pier, and when remonstrated with for his recklessness, coolly asked, " What are ten shillings' worth of passengers compared to spoiling a good race ? " The conveyance of passengers was merely a side-line then, the steamers were run primarily for the purpose of racing one another, and each skipper's object was to get his boat there first, whether full or empty. These boats had served their end as advertisements, albeit at great cost to their owners ; when they went blockade-running they were not replaced, and steamboat-owning on the Clyde came thenceforward to be regarded less as a sport and more as a business proposition.

INTRODUCTORY

"Industry"

The oldest steamer that I can recollect having seen is the "Industry," which was launched from Fife's yard at Fairlie in 1814, just two years after the epoch-making "Comet." She must have been one of the first half-dozen or so of steamers on this side of the Atlantic, and, like all her contemporaries, was of course built of wood. She is said to have been in service up till 1873, but I only knew her as a hulk, lying on the mud in Bowling dock in the eighties. She remained there for a number of years, getting gradually more and more dilapidated, until eventually, when a belated project was put forward for preserving the old relic, the hull was found to be in such a state of decay that nothing could be done. The machinery, however, was preserved and is now in Kelvingrove.

"Inverary Castle"

Photo. by an Amateur

CHAPTER II

HUTCHESON'S VETERANS

OF the boats which I can remember regularly plying the oldest is the

"INVERARAY CASTLE"

Built by Tod & M'Gregor in 1839, she was fitted with the then recently invented steeple engine, one of the many practical ideas of that remarkable genius, David Napier. With her red funnel abaft the paddles, her two masts and fiddle-bow, she was a graceful old craft. Along with her consort, the "Mary Jane," she maintained a daily service between Glasgow and Inveraray, the two boats sailing on alternate mornings, and each making only the single journey in the course of the day. The hour of departure from either end was six o'clock in the morning, and it was often late in the evening ere the boats reached their destination. Both goods and passengers were carried, and a lot of time was put off loading and discharging at the more important piers such as Dunoon, Rothesay and Tarbert. There was an old-world lack of hurry about their methods, and a two hours' stay at Rothesay was no uncommon occurrence, while their progress under steam was of a very leisurely description.

The passenger fares by these boats were not extortionate, for we find the "Inveraray Castle" advertised during the Glasgow Fair holidays of 1879 to carry excursionists from Glasgow to Inveraray and back for four shillings in the cabin and two shillings in the steerage. The advertiser is careful to state that return halves of tickets are not available by the "Columba" or "Iona." These low fares doubtless proved a great boon to Highland people employed in Glasgow, enabling them to enjoy a holiday at home, for at that period labour was not remunerated on any generous scale.

For the whole of her long career the "Inveraray Castle" was employed on the Glasgow-Inveraray station, except for a single season in the late fifties, when, owing to the closing of the Crinan Canal, goods from Glasgow destined for Oban had to be sent round the Mull of Kintyre, and she was placed for the time on that route. After fifty years' service she ceased sailing, and lay for more than one season in Bowling harbour, eventually finding her way into the shipbreakers' hands.

"Mary Jane"

Her consort, the "Mary Jane," came also from Tod & M‘Gregor's yard. Seven years junior to the "Inveraray Castle," she was similar to her in general design, and like her was steeple-engined. It is said that she was built for the Castle Company and originally named "Windsor Castle," but there is no trace in Lloyd's Register of her having ever borne that name. Sir James Matheson, for whom she traded between Glasgow and Stornoway, named her "Mary Jane" in honour of his wife. From his hands the steamer passed into those of D. Hutcheson & Co., and was placed on the Glasgow and Inveraray service, where she plied till 1875. She was then withdrawn and great alterations made in her appearance, the mainmast and bowsprit being removed and the fiddle-bow replaced by a slanting stem. A saloon was erected on the after-deck, and with her name changed to "Glencoe" she took her place on one of the Hebridean routes as a tourist steamer. As such she still plies, although her original engine went to the scrap-heap more than forty years ago, and another steeple-engine of rather less antiquated design now drives her sturdy old clinker-built hull along. During the war she revisited the Firth of Clyde, plying for a short time on the Arran winter service from Ardrossan.

The "Mary Jane" would be the oldest steamer afloat to-day if it were not for the "Glengarry," two years her senior, still at work on Loch Ness. As the "Edinburgh Castle" she was launched by Smith & Rodger seventy-eight years ago, but had left the Clyde many years before our half-century begins. She has been altered beyond recognition since those days, the form of stem and stern having been changed, a saloon added to the after-deck and the funnel shifted from abaft to forward of the paddles, but the original steeple-engine fitted when she was built still keeps her going. Her name, for some reason, has not been included in Lloyd's Register for several years past, but evidently she is not done yet, as three years ago she underwent a complete overhaul, and it would be no surprise if she should survive to complete her century.

So far as I can trace, there are only some half a

dozen steamers afloat to-day that were launched prior to 1850, and no fewer than four of these are old Clyde river-boats. These are, the two already mentioned, the "Glengarry," ex-"Edinburgh Castle," of 1844, and the "Glencoe," ex-"Mary Jane," of 1846, besides the "Premier," also of 1846, built by Denny for the Glasgow and Dumbarton trade, and now forming one of Cosens' fleet at Weymouth, and the "Star," a Tod & M'Gregor boat, launched in 1849 for M'Kellar's Largs and Millport fleet, and now at Nassau in the Bahamas, whither she was sent for blockade-running in the early sixties. The long-continued existence of these old boats surely bears striking testimony to the good material and good workmanship which the Clyde builders of the forties put into their productions. Small wonder, indeed, that our river so early took premier place as an iron shipbuilding centre.

"Iona" No. 3

Messrs D. Hutcheson & Co., the predecessors of Messrs MacBrayne, and owners of the "Inveraray Castle" and "Mary Jane," had also the "Iona" plying between Glasgow and Ardrishaig, the same "Iona" that is still sailing. Her fifty-eight years make her rather venerable as steamships go, though still a comparative juvenile alongside such well-nigh octogenarians as "Glengarry" and "Glencoe." Many people are inclined to be sceptical when told her age, and will remind you that she is by no means the first "Iona"; indeed, there seems to be an impression in some quarters that a new "Iona" is built every

"Glencoe," ex-"Mary Jane"

Photo. by Mr. Dan McDonald, Glasgow

"Iona" No. 3

Photo. by the Author

ten years or so, and the former bearer of the name either relegated to the scrap-heap or sent to other waters under a different name. The idea is, of course, quite a mistaken one, although the present boat is actually the third of the name. The first "Iona," a smart-looking two-funnelled, flush-decked steamer, appeared in 1855 and plied on the Ardrishaig route for eight seasons. There is a beautiful model of this boat in the Kelvingrove Art Galleries. At the end of 1862 season she was sold for blockade-running, but never got away from the Clyde, being run down and sunk in Gourock Bay when on the point of departure. The second "Iona," built to replace her in the following summer, was a saloon steamer, some nine feet shorter than the present boat, but otherwise almost identical. She was very fast, maintaining a speed of eighteen knots from Cloch to Cumbrae when on her trials. This boat only plied for a single season, at the end of which she too was sold for blockade-running. Although she got away from the Clyde, disaster soon overtook her, and she was piled up on Lundy Island on the 2nd of February 1864, and left her bones there.

By that time the third "Iona," the present boat, had already been laid down, and her launch took place in the following May. Her performances on trial were good, although scarcely so fast as those of her predecessor, despite a slight increase of engine-power. On the Ardrishaig run she remained till the advent of the "Columba" in 1878, indeed, she maintained an extra service from the Broomielaw *via* Wemyss Bay during the summer of that year, but that arrangement did not last long, and for some years afterwards we find her running on one of the West Highland tourist routes out of Oban, until another owner had the temerity to start a week-end service to Ardrishaig. The "Iona" was thereupon brought round to the Clyde and placed on a daily service from Ardrishaig in the mornings and from the Broomielaw at half-past one in the afternoon, an arrangement which was continued after the interloper had withdrawn from the station. Since that time the "Iona" has remained on the Clyde. During the war she ran for a season for the Caledonian Steam Packet Co. on the Wemyss Bay route to Rothesay, and in the past summer she sailed with success between the Broomielaw and Lochgoilhead. She is interesting as the last of the regular Clyde boats carrying the old, narrow deck saloons with alleyways along the bulwarks. She bears her years lightly and is still a handsome boat, and, while not exactly a greyhound now, can still attain a very respectable speed.

The "Iona" only plied during the summer months, and during the winter the Ardrishaig trade was maintained by the "Mountaineer."

"Mountaineer" No. 1

This smart little two-funnelled boat, flush-decked and steeple-engined, had been built in 1852, indeed, she was the pioneer boat of the Ardrishaig route when it was opened in that year. Like many other flush-decked steamers, she was afterwards fitted with a deck saloon. The "Mountaineer" was practically an all-the-year-round boat, sailing out of Oban during the

HUTCHESON'S VETERANS 15

summer, while the "Iona" and "Columba" were in commission. Just before the close of the summer season of 1889 she was totally lost by stranding in the Sound of Mull.

"CHEVALIER"

Sometimes, when the "Mountaineer" was withdrawn for overhauling, the carrying-on of the winter service to Ardrishaig was entrusted to the "Chevalier," a vessel of similar design to the "Iona," but smaller and two years her junior. For the most part, however, her voyagings were made among the lochs and isles on the other side of the Kintyre peninsula, with Oban for her head-quarters. In the summer of 1913, after the withdrawal of the "Edinburgh Castle," the "Chevalier" was placed for a time on the Glasgow and Lochgoilhead station, and during the war remained on the Clyde and helped to eke out the scanty service of that period. After the Armistice, she resumed her sailings with mails and passengers between Oban and Crinan, and still continues to ply.

All of these steamers, the three "Ionas," the "Mountaineer" and the "Chevalier," were built by J. & G. Thomson at Govan, and the engines of all save the "Mountaineer" were of oscillating type.

The Broomielaw in the Seventies
with "Viceroy" (left), "Guinevere" (centre) and "Vesta" (right)

Photo. by Messrs. G. W. Wilson & Co. Aberdeen; now Mr. Fred. W. Hardie)

CHAPTER III

SAILINGS FROM THE BROOMIELAW

THERE were already a number of railway services to the coast in 1872, although the Fairlie, Craigendoran and Gourock routes and the Caledonian route to Arran by Ardrossan had not been opened. The Wemyss Bay and Prince's Pier services, as well as the South-Western Ardrossan-Arran service, were in full operation, while the Caledonian Co. ran connections from Greenock old quay, and the North British Co. maintained a service to Dunoon and the lochs from Helensburgh pier.

But the main bulk of the traffic still went from the Broomielaw, and it was possible in those days to sail all the way to destinations that can now be reached only by rail or by a combination of rail and steamer.

" GUINEVERE "

Thus, the day-tripper to Arran could step on board the " Guinevere " at the Broomielaw at eight o'clock in the morning, and travel by way of Greenock, Dunoon, Rothesay and Kilchattan Bay to Corrie, Brodick and Lamlash, returning by the same route and reaching Glasgow shortly after eight in the evening. The " Guinevere " was a two-funnelled steamer of raised-quarterdeck design, and of moderate speed, built in 1869 by Duncan of Port-Glasgow, and fitted by Rankin & Blackmore with a pair of oscillating engines which worked very smoothly and took up little space. Her original owners were Graham, Brymner & Co., but she passed through various hands and sported more varieties of funnel-painting than any other steamer I have known, remaining, however, on the Arran station until bought by Captain Buchanan in 1884. He transferred her to the Broomielaw-Rothesay run, on which she continued to trade until sold to the Turks in 1892. She sailed for Constantinople, but never reached her destination, and all that we can say of her is :—

"She's gone, and none save Wind and Wave can tell the when and how,
And them that watched the lists for her, they're tired o' watchin' now;
Far down, far down in Deadman's Bay both ship and men do lie,
And the Lutine bell has rung for her this many a day gone by."

There were also steamers to Ayr in those days, where the "Vale of Clwyd" and successive "Bonnie Doons" maintained a service, until the increasing railway facilities to the "Auld Toon" rendered the steamboat trade unprofitable, and it ended with the withdrawal and sale of the last "Bonnie Doon" in 1881. These boats belonged to Messrs Seath & Steel, and were all built at Seath's yard in Rutherglen.

SAILINGS FROM THE BROOMIELAW

"Vale of Clwyd"

The "Vale of Clwyd," although dating only from 1865, was of the old-fashioned design in vogue in the fifties, with the funnel abaft the paddles. Her machinery was of a peculiar type, the main engine being a steeple, in combination with a small diagonal. In the summer of 1877 she was chartered by Messrs Campbell & Gillies, to replace the lost "Lady Gertrude" on the Wemyss Bay route until the "Adela," which was building to replace her, should be ready. After that, the "Vale of Clwyd" traded for a time between Glasgow, Largs and Millport, and in 1881 was sent to the Thames, where she ran for a number of years under her original name.

"Bonnie Doon" No. 1

Of the first "Bonnie Doon," built in 1870, I have but the faintest recollection, but she appears to have had the funnel forward of the paddles and a short deck saloon aft. Her career on the Clyde cannot have exceeded two or three seasons at most, and she went to Stettin, where she remained for a long time, under the name of "Kronprinz Friedrich Wilhelm." The second "Bonnie Doon" was not built till 1876; I shall refer to her later, when dealing with the steamers of that year.

The Campbeltown boats were the "Gael" and the "Kintyre," built by Robertson of Greenock in 1867 and 1868 respectively.

"Gael"

The "Gael," a handsome paddle-boat of some 400 tons, with two funnels and two masts, was far more like a small channel steamer than a river-boat, her draught of water being nearly double that of the craft plying on the upper firth. Sold in the early eighties to ply in English waters, she was bought a few years later by Messrs MacBrayne, and has long been a familiar figure in all the ports that lie between Oban and Portree. During the war she lay for some time in Bowling harbour, and after an overhaul on the slip at Port-Glasgow, took up some of the Firth of Clyde sailings, but in 1920 resumed her Hebridean voyagings. Some changes have been made in her appearance, including the erection of a large forecastle, but none of them sufficient to cause any difficulty in identifying her. Her engines, of non-compound oscillating type, are those fitted into her by Rankin & Blackmore when she was built, but a surface-condenser has been added to her original equipment.

"Kintyre"

The "Kintyre" was a screw-steamer, one of the prettiest little models ever turned out on the Clyde, or anywhere for that matter. Her fine lines, although limiting her carrying capacity, combined with her graceful clipper bow and the smart rake of her masts and funnel to give her more the appearance of a private yacht than a trading vessel. Her speed was but moderate, however, and she was not always kept in

"Gael"

Photo by an Amateur

the smart condition that her graceful lines seemed to merit. Her end came some fifteen years ago, when she was run down and sunk in broad daylight, off Skelmorlie, by a new steamer running her trials. Unfortunately, the accident was attended with some loss of life.

"SULTAN"

The Kyles of Bute traffic was in the hands of Captain Alexander Williamson, sen., who had placed the "Sultan" on the route in 1862. Built in the previous year, this handy little boat had spent her first season on the Kilmun station before coming into Captain Williamson's hands. She had the old-fashioned slanting stem and square stern, and was fitted with a steeple engine which had already done duty on board an older steamer named the "Wellington." The "Sultan" sailed for Captain Williamson for about thirty years before being sold with the rest of his fleet to the Glasgow and South-Western Railway Co. Her bow having met with an accident which necessitated some repairs, the opportunity was taken to fit her with a straight stem. She did not remain long with the Railway Co., and we next encounter her as the "Ardmore," sailing for Captain John Williamson, son of her former owner, but her stay with him was even shorter, and she was acquired by Messrs MacBrayne to run on the Caledonian Canal. Shortened to fit the locks, equipped with full deck saloons fore and aft, and again re-named, this time the "Gairlochy," she continued to ply between Banavie and Inverness for nearly a quarter of a century, until her career was ended by an outbreak of fire which occurred on board her when lying at Fort-Augustus one night in the last week of December 1919. So suddenly did the flames spread that the crew had scarcely time to scramble ashore, but fortunately all succeeded in reaching safety, although all their effects were lost. I last saw the burnt-out shell of the old steamer in the summer of 1920, lying in Loch Ness, just outside the locks at Fort-Augustus.

" SULTANA "

The name of the " Sultana " stands out prominently in the list of Clyde steamers. Built for Captain Williamson by Robertson of Greenock in 1868, and fitted with a diagonal engine by Wm. King & Co., she was an invaluable asset in establishing a traffic for the South-Western Co. by the Prince's Pier route which they opened in 1869. Her straight stem and knife-like entrance, with the rake of mast and funnel and the sweeping curve of her paddle-box, conveyed to the beholder an impression of speed which her performances did not fail to bear out. Though her engine was not particularly powerful, she had a very rapid stroke and travelled at a great pace, her fine lines offering no resistance to the water. Though rather crank with a big crowd on board, she steered beautifully when in proper trim; few Clyde steamers have equalled, and certainly none have excelled her in manœuvring at piers. She was commanded in turn by Captain Williamson, sen., and his three sons, James, Alexander and John, all of whom showed great skill in availing themselves to the utmost of her speed and handiness. During the

"Sultana"

Photo. by Messrs. J. Adamson & Son, Rothesay

SAILINGS FROM THE BROOMIELAW

seventies the competition between the Prince's Pier and Wemyss Bay routes for the Rothesay traffic was exceptionally keen, and as a fast boat was always certain to secure her share of it, especially on the morning up run and the evening down run, the "Sultana" bore an important part in the contest. She left Port Bannatyne each morning at 7.10, and Rothesay at 7.32, calling at Innellan and thence direct to Prince's Pier, where she lay till 10.50, connecting then with the 10.5 train from St Enoch and running to Rothesay via Kirn, Dunoon and Innellan. From Rothesay she sailed on excursions to Ormidale and round the Island of Bute on alternate days, returning in time to take the three o'clock up run. She left Prince's Pier again in connection with the 4.5 afternoon train, direct for Innellan, Rothesay and Port Bannatyne, where her day's work ended. Dunoon and Kirn passengers on the morning up and afternoon down runs were carried by the "Sultan." Although the shorter sail via Wemyss Bay gave that route an advantage, enabling the distance between Glasgow and Rothesay to be covered in less time, yet the prowess of the little "Sultana" appealed so strongly to many of the daily travellers that she never lacked a fair complement of passengers, enthusiastic partisans who would not travel by any other boat so long as she was available.

"Sultana," like "Sultan," passed successively to the South-Western Railway Co. and to Captain John Williamson. By the Railway Co. she was employed principally on the Holy Loch run. Captain Williamson placed her in the Broomielaw-Rothesay trade, where she plodded along for a few years like an old racehorse reduced to the cab-rank. About the end of the century she was sold to France, and has now disappeared from Lloyd's Register. It is generally conceded that she holds the record from Prince's Pier to Rothesay by the usual route *via* Kirn, Dunoon and Innellan, having covered the distance in fifty-seven minutes from pier to pier.

The Holy Loch traffic was cared for by Captain Bob Campbell with the " Vivid " and the " Vesta."

" Vivid "

The " Vivid," built for him by Barclay, Curle & Co. in 1864, with a steeple engine by her builders, was a smart and popular boat, and bore his colours, all-white funnel and black hull, with green underbody, on the Kilmun station for more than twenty years. Towards the end of 1884 she was transferred to Buchanan's Broomielaw-Rothesay trade, on which she remained for the rest of her days. The " Vivid " has the distinction of being the last steeple-engined steamer plying regularly on the Firth. The type is almost obsolete everywhere now; it still survives in the " Glengarry " and " Glencoe," and in the " Star " at Nassau, but I am not aware of any others. The last time I saw the " Vivid " was late in 1902. She was then lying in the Pudzeoch at Renfrew, partly dismantled, in course of being broken up.

" Vesta "

The " Vesta " had been bought in by Captain Campbell, having originally formed one of the old

M'Kellar Largs and Millport fleet. She was one of the boats that had remained on the Clyde during blockade times, having come from Barr's yard in 1853. Withdrawn from the Kilmun route in the late seventies, she traded to Garelochhead for Hugh Keith and afterwards for Captain Buchanan. A tubby-bowed little craft of antiquated design, steeple-engined and wearing her funnel abaft the paddles, never even in her best days an outstanding boat, it cannot have occasioned much loss to anyone when she was totally destroyed by fire at Ardenadam pier one autumn night in 1886.

" Carrick Castle "

The Glasgow and Lochgoil Steamboat Co., under the management of Mr M. T. Clark, had a fine steamer called the " Carrick Castle," which they had got from Fullerton of Paisley in 1870, the only paddle-steamer built by this firm for the Firth traffic. Her engines, by Wm. King & Co., were of diagonal type, similar to those of " Sultana," and in general dimensions she approximated closely to that steamer. Wearing the attractive red funnel with black and white bands, still borne by the " Lord of the Isles," she looked very smart and had a good turn of speed.

For many seasons the " Carrick Castle " made a regular Saturday evening excursion during July and August to Gourock and back, leaving the Broomielaw at half-past five and arriving back about ten o'clock. The return fares on these occasions were ninepence in the cabin and sixpence in the steerage.

In 1881 she went to the Firth of Forth, and two years

afterwards I saw her at the Isle of May, whither she had conveyed a party of excursionists. After that she appeared on the Bristol Channel, bearing in succession the names of " Lady Margaret " and " Lord Tredegar " : at that point I lose sight of her and am inclined to think she had been scrapped.

EMBARKING AT THE BROOMIELAW, GLASGOW. 5066.

Broomielaw about 1885

with "Chancellor" (3), "Vivid," "Eagle" and "Guinevere," reading from the spectator. One of the original "Cluthas," on left.

Photo, by Messrs. G. W. Wilson, & Co., Aberdeen (now Mr. Fred W. Hardie)

CHAPTER IV

MORE SAILINGS FROM THE BROOMIELAW

BUT the greatest volume of traffic was on the Rothesay route, where, in addition to the Hutcheson and Williamson boats, were the fleets of Buchanan, Stewart, M'Lean and some others. The Hutcheson boats passed to Messrs MacBrayne, and the Buchanan and Williamson interests are now combined; the remainder have long since gone out of business.

"EAGLE"

Buchanan's "Eagle," built in 1864 to replace a former steamer of the name which had gone off blockade-running, was a long steamer of raised-quarterdeck design, with a double diagonal engine, constructed by the Anchor Line. Charles Connell & Co. were the builders of the hull. This steamer had originally two funnels, placed forward of the paddles, and though by no means a beauty, was a comfortable and popular boat, and while not exactly a greyhound, attained quite a respectable speed. The original engine did not give satisfaction, and in 1876 it was removed, and later placed in a new hull called the "Brodick Castle," where it gave better results, and the "Eagle" was refitted with a single diagonal engine by Wm. King & Co.

After this overhaul she reappeared with a single funnel. The newspaper advertisements of her sailings in 1876 were headed " Observe, ' Eagle ' renewed."

For the greater part of her career on the Clyde, she plied between the Broomielaw and Rothesay, but for a few years from 1886 onward her voyages were extended to Arran, a long, narrow saloon having been superimposed on her already raised quarterdeck. In this arrangement she is unique among Clyde steamers ; it gave her rather a topheavy appearance, but even with the erection she was in reality a good, stable boat. On the opening of the Manchester Ship Canal in 1894 the " Eagle " was sent there with the object of opening up a passenger trade, but the experiment was not a success, and before long the old steamer had found her way to the shipbreakers at Liverpool. A panel which once formed part of her fitting, now fitted into the woodwork in the saloon of the " Eagle III.," survives as a relic of the veteran.

" Rothesay Castle "

Buchanan's other steamer, the " Rothesay Castle," put into the water at Renfrew by Henderson in 1865, was a flush-decked, steeple-engined boat, with two funnels in the orthodox fore-and-aft style. After a number of years on the Rothesay run, she was placed on the Ardrossan-Arran service, when Captain Buchanan took it over in January 1874. There she remained until the winter of 1878–79, being then sold and sent to France. She has long since disappeared from Lloyd's Register, but a Glasgow gentleman, formerly closely

"Eagle" at the Broomielaw about 1865
"Vesta" on left

Photo. by Messrs. T. & R. Annan & Sons, Glasgow

connected with the river steamboat traffic, informs me that he ran across her on a French river not so very many years ago.

"LORNE"

Stewart's boats were the "Undine" and the "Lorne." The latter, the only boat ever built by M'Millan of Dumbarton for the river fleet, was a handsome, two-funnelled, flush-decked steamer. Her engines, of diagonal oscillating pattern, were the work of J. & J. Thomson. A fast boat, big as steamers ruled then, she was quite an acquisition to the Clyde fleet, but her healthy appetite for coal accorded but ill with her owner's economical tastes, so that, when a favourable opportunity presented itself at the end of her second season, she was sold to Danish owners, and sent to Copenhagen, where she was long known as the "Oresund."

"UNDINE"

The "Undine," a product of Henderson's Renfrew yard in 1865, was flush-decked and diagonal-engined, with a single funnel forward of the paddles. She was usually run in leisurely fashion, but could evidently reach a fair speed when pressed, as we learn from the newspapers of 23rd April 1868 that "Yesterday afternoon the steamers 'Undine' and 'Eagle,' leaving Glasgow at three and four o'clock respectively, reached Greenock quay in ninety minutes." The "Undine" was a very crank boat, listing over at the slightest provocation. My last recollection of her is of seeing her from the deck of another steamer off Toward Point, with her sponson under water and a cataract pouring from the vents in her particularly handsome paddle-box. She disappeared from the Clyde about the beginning of 1879, and I know nothing of her subsequent history.

"Elaine."

When he sold the "Lorne," Captain Stewart bought in a small steamer called the "Elaine," a comfortable boat of raised-quarterdeck design, but not by any means speedy. She had been built by R. Duncan & Co. at Port-Glasgow in 1867 and had a nice little pair of oscillating engines by Rankin & Blackmore. Her original owners were Graham, Brymner & Co., but she had already passed through other hands before Captain Stewart got her. Her paddle-boxes were very small, the tops of them coming only a few inches above the hurricane deck. One peculiarity of her appearance was her very short steam-pipe, which only reached about halfway up the funnel. After the sale of the "Undine," Captain Stewart ran the "Elaine" alone for a few months and then sold her to Captain Buchanan and retired from the business altogether. For her new owner the "Elaine" plied for about twenty years on the Broomielaw-Rothesay and Broomielaw-Garelochhead routes. In his hands she was fitted with bigger paddle-boxes and a steam-pipe of ordinary length. At the end of 1899 season this steamer was broken up at Bowling.

Captain Sandy M'Lean, a well-known figure on the

"Elaine"

Photo, by Messrs. J. Adamson & Son, Rothesay

"Marquis of Bute" at the Broomielaw
with "Lord of the Isles" (1) beyond; "Benmore" in mid-river;
"Dunoon Castle" and "Vivid" on left

Photo. by Messrs. Valentine & Sons, Dundee

SAILINGS FROM THE BROOMIELAW 31

Firth, owned at the time of my earliest recollections two steamers called the "Marquis of Bute" and the "Vulcan."

"Vulcan"

The latter was a small steamer, built in 1854, with her funnel aft, and her engines were of oscillating type. Her original owners were Messrs Napier, who built and engined her, and for whom Captain M'Lean had sailed as her skipper. After being sold out of his service in 1872, the "Vulcan," which had become the property of Messrs J. & G. Thomson, the shipbuilders, was employed as a conveyance for their workers between the Broomielaw and the new shipyard at Clydebank. I can well remember seeing her come alongside the quay on her upward journey one evening. No gangway was required to accommodate her passengers; all along her length they climbed on the bulwarks and scrambled up the quay-wall, and before she was even moored the boat was empty. When the railway to Clydebank was opened the "Vulcan's" services were no longer required and she went to the scrap-heap.

"Marquis of Bute"

The "Marquis of Bute" was one of Barclay, Curle's happiest productions. She was of very similar dimensions to the "Sultana" launched by Robertson in the same year, and like her, was diagonal-engined. Like her, too, she combined the very desirable qualities of economy and speed; her paddles had not the same rapid beat, but the stroke of every float was much more powerful. The "Marquis" was the morning boat from Rothesay, sailing at 7.5 a.m., *via* Innellan, Dunoon and Kirn and running direct from Greenock to Glasgow. How fast she was may be judged from the fact that it was no uncommon thing for her to put her passengers ashore at the Broomielaw, then cant, and be lying moored with her head downstream before ten o'clock. Apart from this, however, she got little chance of showing her powers, for Captain M'Lean evinced a very strong distaste for racing, and it was only after the "Marquis" went into the hands of Captain Williamson in the late eighties that she ever was fairly matched against other boats. Even then, the latest productions of the yards found great difficulty in shaking off the veteran.

This is the first steamer that I can recall as having run on evening cruises. They were not known by that name then, but simply as "pleasure trips." The "Marquis's" regular day's run being over before five o'clock, Captain M'Lean often arranged little evening trips from Rothesay to Loch Striven or Ormidale or round Bute. The advertising of these was entrusted to the Rothesay bellman. Dressed in a blue coat with brass buttons, that functionary used to march round the front in the forenoon, stopping every now and then to ring the bell and announce :

"Notice! The fine steamer 'Marquis of Bute' will sail this evenin', weather permittin', on a pleeasure excursion to the Head of Loch Struvvin. Leaving Rothesay about five o'clock. Calling at Port Bannatyne, goin' and returnin'. Fares : Cabin, ninepence ; steerage, sixpence."

SAILINGS FROM THE BROOMIELAW

M'Lean, though not refined, was a kind-hearted man, a rough diamond, but a diamond all the same, and if at the advertised hour of starting the steamer was not full, he would sometimes invite the newsboys from the quay to come on board, pack them in the bows with strict injunctions to " bide there and behave themselves," and take them for a gratis trip. Needless to say, he was a very popular personage with the newsboys. Owing to the absence of piers on the shores of Loch Striven, there was no regular steamboat service there, and the public owed a debt of gratitude to Captain M'Lean for giving them the opportunity of viewing the varied beauties of this delightful Highland loch.

As stated, the " Marquis " joined the Williamson fleet, in which she remained for a few years, until it was sold *en bloc* to the South-Western Railway Co. in 1891. They placed her on the Fairlie-Millport run, and she continued there for about a dozen years. Then, after a season or two under charter on Belfast Lough, she returned to the Clyde in the late autumn of 1906. I am uncertain whether she was then broken up or sent to other waters.

" Athole "

The " Athole," like the " Marquis," was a Barclay, Curle boat, of much the same size but of raised-quarter-deck design and steeple-engined. Built for Captain Stewart in 1866, she evidently did not remain long in his possession. The South-Western Railway Co. bought her to run in connection with their trains to Prince's Pier in the early seventies, but ere long she went into Captain M'Lean's hands to replace the " Vulcan." A comfortable, well-constructed boat, though not fast, it was quite a pity when, on M'Lean's stoppage, the lack of demand for steamers of her class caused her to be laid up, and after lying unemployed for some years, sent to the shipbreakers.

"Ardencaple," "Ardgowan" and "Levan"

Three very small paddle steamers, the smallest that have plied on the Clyde during these fifty years, had been launched for Graham, Brymner & Co. from three separate yards at Port-Glasgow in 1866. R. Duncan & Co. were the builders of the "Ardencaple"; Laurence, Hill & Co., of the "Ardgowan"; and Blackwood & Gordon, of the "Levan." Rankin & Blackmore supplied oscillating engines for these steamers. The boats, which were of raised-quarterdeck design, were all of the same size, but differed from one another in minor details. They registered a good deal less than one hundred tons gross. Originally placed in the Gareloch trade, they did not prove remunerative, and in 1875 we find the "Levan" sailing to Lochgoilhead. About the end of that season all three were sent to the Thames.

"Craigrownie"

With them went the "Craigrownie," a larger steamer of the same type, in many respects a sister-ship to the "Elaine," her builders and engineers being the same. She had made her debut in 1870 and seen service on various Clyde routes. Her last employment here was between the Broomielaw and Millport, leaving Glasgow at ten minutes from ten in the morning, and returning

"Athole"

Photo. by Messrs. J. Adamson & Son, Rothesay

SAILINGS FROM THE BROOMIELAW 35

at three o'clock in the afternoon, with calls at Kilcreggan, Dunoon and Largs. As Lloyd's Register does not concern itself with steamers under one hundred tons, it is not easy to trace the further history of the three smaller boats, although I know that the "Ardencaple" was still afloat in 1886. "Craigrownie's" career is more easily followed, as she measured over one hundred tons. She was plying on the Thames as the "Duke of Edinburgh" as late as 1895.

"Lancelot"

The same builders and engineers were responsible for the "Lancelot," a similar vessel to the "Craigrownie" and "Elaine," but rather larger, which had been built in 1868. She also was owned by Messrs Graham, Brymner & Co., who employed her on the Largs and Millport station. In 1875 this boat was bought by Messrs Campbell & Gillies for the Wemyss Bay trade, to replace the "Venus," which had been broken up. She was a useful boat to her new owners, running to all the ports served from Wemyss Bay, and was often used for short excursions from the coast towns, for which she proved very well suited. As in the case of the "Elaine," her paddle-boxes, originally very small, were replaced with larger ones, doubtless with a view to render easier the embarking and disembarking of passengers at low water. Her connection with the Wemyss Bay route lasted until Campbell & Gillies went out of business in 1890. Shortly after that she was sent to Constantinople, where she bore the name of "Erenkieui," but is no longer to be traced.

Wemyss Bay Pier and Fleet about 1875
with (left to right) "Largs," "Lancelot," "Lady Gertrude," and "Argyle."

Photo. by Messrs. J. Adamson & Son, Rothesay

CHAPTER V

RAILWAY STEAMERS

OF the railway routes then existing, the Caledonian from Greenock old quay, and the South-Western from Prince's Pier, relied on connections with the up-river boats. The South-Western, indeed, had at one time bought in the "Athole" and "Craigrownie" to maintain their service, but this arrangement did not last long. The Wemyss Bay and Helensburgh services, as well as the service between Ardrossan and Arran, were carried on by boats specially employed.

Those on the Wemyss Bay run were owned by Messrs Campbell & Gillies, and consisted of the "Argyle," "Largs," "Venus" and "Lady Gertrude."

"ARGYLE"

The "Argyle" had been built for Captain Stewart by Barclay, Curle & Co. in 1866, and had the steeple-engine of one of his earlier steamers, the "Alma," fitted into her. After fourteen years' service she was re-engined on the same principle. With a beautifully modelled hull, she was an excellent sea-boat, very lively, but very dry, not fast, but an invaluable boat for the winter service. When the Wemyss Bay Steamboat Co. gave up business, she went to Dundee and plied on the Tay for many years before going under the shipbreaker's hammer.

"Venus"

The "Venus" and the "Largs" were small two-funnelled steamers. The "Venus," which was steeple-engined, had originally formed one of the M'Kellar fleet, for which she had been built by J. & G. Thomson in 1852, and had been commanded there by Captain Gillies, who bought her for himself when M'Kellar gave up business. When Captain Gillies and his son-in-law, Captain Campbell, undertook the Wemyss Bay service, they placed the "Venus" on it, and she remained there for some years. I have but a very faint recollection of this boat, but can remember, as a small boy, looking from the window of a coast train and having a dismantled hulk pointed out to me, which, I was told, was the old "Venus," in course of being broken up. That was probably at Port-Glasgow, and the date must have been about 1874.

"Largs"

The "Largs" had been built by Messrs T. Wingate & Co. for the Wemyss Bay Railway Co. in 1864, in anticipation of the opening of the railway in the following year. Along with two bigger boats, the "Kyles" and the "Bute," which had been got from Caird, she opened the service, which, however, turned out very unprofitable at first. The Railway Co. soon tired of steamboat-owning, and the "Kyles" and "Bute" were sold to the Thames, where the "Bute," re-named "Princess Alice," had a tragic end. Coming up the river one evening at the end of September 1878 with a large complement of excursionists, she was run into and sunk

"Lady Gertrude"

From an Old Photograph

by the collier " Bywell Castle." The disaster, one of the greatest in the history of river navigation, involved the loss of between five hundred and six hundred lives. The " Largs " remained in the Wemyss Bay service after Campbell & Gillies took it over, her regular run being on the Largs and Millport section. At the end of 1876 season she left the Clyde, to ply for many years at Waterford under the name of " Mermaid."

" LADY GERTRUDE "

The " Lady Gertrude " was built and engined by Blackwood & Gordon, and was of about the same size as the " Sultana," " Marquis of Bute " and " Carrick Castle," and, like them, was propelled by a diagonal engine. She never had, however, the smart appearance of these boats. Some ten years ago, in looking over an old newspaper file of 1872, I came accidentally on the account of her launch. The good wishes expressed at that function for " Success to the ' Lady Gertrude ' " were, unfortunately, not destined to be realised, and her whole lifetime did not extend to five years. When she was going alongside Toward pier one afternoon in the winter of 1876, the engine failed to reverse, with the result that she went on the rocks and became a wreck. Her boiler, lying on the shore, was a landmark for a number of years ; the engine, however, was salved and fitted into the new steamer " Adela " in the following year.

" DANDIE DINMONT " No. 1

The North British Railway Co. started steamboat-owning on the Firth in 1866. Their first steamers were two handsome and expensive saloon boats, built and engined by Messrs A. & J. Inglis. The engines were diagonal with two cranks. These boats ran at first to Dunoon, Rothesay and Ardrishaig, but their owners' experience was similar to that of the Wemyss Bay Co. One of the boats, the " Meg Merrilies," was sold off the river ; the other, the " Dandie Dinmont," had her run curtailed and did not sail farther than Dunoon and the Holy Loch. Her skipper, Captain John M'Kinlay, in October 1876 received from the residents of Kilcreggan and the Holy Loch villages a gift of a purse of sovereigns and a mantelpiece clock, in recognition of various occasions on which he had been instrumental in rescuing people from drowning. The presentation was made on board the steamer at Sandbank.

There is a beautiful model of one of these boats in Kelvingrove. It shows the old colours, red funnel with black top, and white paddle-boxes which distinguished the North British boats until exchanged for the present colours in 1883. The "Dandie Dinmont" sailed on the Clyde till 1887, when she was sold to South of England owners.

" Gareloch "

In 1872 a small, raised-quarterdeck steamer called the " Gareloch " was built for the North British Co. by Henry Murray & Co., to ply between Helensburgh and Garelochhead. Her oscillating engines were by D. Rowan & Co. After about twenty years' service she was transferred to the Firth of Forth, to form one of the Galloway fleet. One day in the summer of 1895, as I was sailing down past the Forth Bridge, I noticed

RAILWAY STEAMERS

a paddle-steamer in the distance, which I at once set down as a product of one or other of that long line of shipyards which then stretched from Caird's at Greenock to Tommy Seath's at Ru'glen. When she came alongside, notwithstanding that she was painted in the Galloway colours and bore the name " Wemyss Castle," I had no difficulty in recognising the old " Gareloch."

"Chancellor" No. 2

From Helensburgh there also sailed a steamer of very peculiar design, named the " Chancellor," a Blackwood & Gordon boat, built in 1864. Her run was to Arrochar, and in the height of the season she made two double journeys each day. She was designed on the model of one of the Loch Lomond steamers, the " Prince Consort," which had appeared a year or two before, with deck saloons fore and aft, and sponsons carried right round to stem and stern, giving a very large deck space. All her passenger accommodation was above the main-deck; in fact, her hull was merely a sort of canoe, to support the sponsons and deck-houses. She had a small pair of diagonal engines and did not carry a mast. After sailing for sixteen years on Loch Long, she made way for a new steamer of the same name. Her own name was changed to " Shandon," and she became one of Hugh Keith's fleet on the Gareloch. Captain Buchanan was her next owner, the Keith fleet having been purchased by him in 1884. The " Shandon " sailed for him from the Broomielaw, sometimes to Rothesay and sometimes to the Gareloch. A mast had meanwhile been placed in her, for convenience in carrying a light.

On the opening of the Manchester canal the "Shandon" was sent there and renamed "Daniel Adamson," in honour of the chairman of the Canal company. As already mentioned, the attempt to establish a passenger trade on the Canal proved abortive, so the steamer came back to the Clyde. A few weeks' experience sufficed to show that she was by that time hopelessly behind the times, and she soon went to the knackers.

On the occasion of the launch of the steamship "City of New York" in March 1888 I went down to Clydebank by the "Shandon." It was a cold day, and a snell wind with snow in it blew directly up the river. After the launch had taken place the "Shandon" proceeded to turn round for the homeward journey, but the pressure of the wind on the big surface presented by her saloons, which her shallow draught was insufficient to resist, immediately forced her back to her original position. After repeated unsuccessful attempts, she was, as a last resource, backed up to Messrs Lobnitz' slip at Renfrew and canted there by means of a hawser fastened to a pawl.

"The Lady Mary"

The Ardrossan-Arran boats, "The Lady Mary" and the "Heather Bell," were run by the Duke of Hamilton's trustees. Both were flush-decked steamers by Blackwood & Gordon, and their dates of launching were 1868 and 1871. "The Lady Mary," a short two-funnelled boat with oscillating engines, had nothing sensational about her.

"Daniel Adamson," ex-"Shandon," ex-"Chancellor" (2), leaving the Broomielaw
"Benmore" alongside quay, "Iona" canting.

Photo. by Messrs T. & R. Annan & Sons, Glasgow

"HEATHER BELL"

The "Heather Bell's" career on the Arran station was brief and brilliant. Driven by a pair of diagonal engines of great power, she is said to have established a record between Ardrossan and Brodick that stood undisturbed till the days of the turbine, but she was a most extravagant coal-eater. The Duke's trustees soon grew tired of seeing all the purser's takings and something over rolling out at the top of her big black funnel, and at the beginning of 1874 they retired from the business and sold the boats, "The Lady Mary" going to the Bristol Channel and the "Heather Bell" to the south of England. The "Heather Bell" came back to the Clyde in 1900 and ran for a short time in the Sunday trade. On the withdrawal of the Hamilton trustees, Captain Buchanan assumed control of the Ardrossan-Arran traffic and maintained it until the Railway Co. put on their own boats in 1892.

CHAPTER VI

VARIOUS BOATS

THERE were several other steamers running on the Firth, whose exact stations I cannot recall; some, indeed, did not remain long on any one route.

" HERO "

One of these was the " Hero," a longish boat with the funnel abaft the paddles. I find that in 1875 she was running daily between Glasgow and Rothesay, starting downward at 11.45 and returning at 4.30. Evidently she was doing no good, for in the newspapers of 25th August of that year there figures under the heading " Vessels for Sale " the following notice :—

" The well-known steamer ' Hero ' of 70 tons register and 80 horse-power, presently plying upon the Clyde. Built and engined with superior steeple engines by Thomas Wingate & Co. in 1858. Has certificate for 753 passengers, is a swift boat and light in fuel."

Whether a sale was effected I am unable to trace, but in the newspapers of 10th September following she is advertised to sail between Glasgow and Rothesay, carrying steerage passengers at sixpence for the single journey. It must have been somewhere about this period that the " Hero " passed into the hands of Hugh

Keith, and it may have been for him that she sailed on the Arran run in the summer of 1878. She was afterwards placed in his Gareloch service. Captain Buchanan, who acquired her in 1884, retained her as a spare boat and sold her about 1890 to Messrs MacBrayne, who wanted a steamer to replace the " Mountaineer." They transferred that name to her and rejuvenated her, fitting her with a deck saloon and a handsome clipper bow, and she plied regularly out of Oban until broken up about 1907.

" Marquis of Lorne "

The " Marquis of Lorne," originally Stewart's " Victory," was built and engined by Barclay, Curle in 1863, and, being one of the few good boats on the river in that year, had made some money for her owner. She was almost a sister-ship to the " Argyle," though slightly smaller, and after leaving Captain Stewart's possession, was associated with that steamer for a short time in the Campbell & Gillies fleet. By the time I knew her she had got rather down at heel, being owned by a certain Duncan Dewar, who ran her seven days a week. This steamer, under her third and last name of " Cumbrae," was the first to be placed by Messrs Hill & Co. on the Fairlie route when it was opened in 1882, and remained on it until the South-Western Co. placed their own boats on the station in 1892. She seems to have lain unemployed for some years, and was eventually dismantled and sent to Newry as a coal-hulk.

"Balmoral"

Photo. lent by Messrs. Buchanan Steamers, Ltd.

"Balmoral"

The "Balmoral," employed in Keith's Gareloch trade, was a very old boat, short and with the funnel behind the engine-house. Launched as the "Lady Brisbane" in 1842, when steam navigation on the Clyde was only thirty years old, she was originally intended to oppose the M'Kellar boats on the Largs and Millport run, but before long an arrangement was come to, and she was running in conjunction with them. In her early days she was looked upon as very fast, so much so that the public were timorous about travelling by her. An experimental boat, called the "Telegraph," with a non-condensing engine working at high pressure, had blown up with fatal effects in the previous year, and had created a scare, so that it was found necessary to insert in the advertisements of the "Lady Brisbane's" sailings a statement to the effect that her engine and boiler were of safe construction and not on the high pressure principle. The "Balmoral" went into the Buchanan fleet with the rest of the Keith boats, and was running till the early nineties, succumbing eventually to a sort of heart attack following over-exertion. Chased down the Gareloch by one of the fliers of the day, the old boat had succeeded in reaching Helensburgh pier first, but on the subsequent run to Greenock something went wrong, the inquisitive little crosshead of her steeple engine rose to take a last fond look from its observation box on the hurricane-deck, and then, with a clatter of metal, the whole contrivance collapsed on the bed-plate. The engine, like the deacon's famous one-hoss shay, had

> " Gone to pieces all at once,
> All at once and nothing fust,
> Just like bubbles when they bust."

Inspection showed that the damage was beyond repair, so the scrap of the machinery was shovelled out, and the little dismantled hull sent over to Ireland and moored as a coal-hulk in the mudflats of Newry river.

One day, about seventeen years ago, I sailed up the Newry canal on the bridge of a small coasting steamer, and looking across the narrow trickle of the river I noticed two old vessels on the opposite side, serving in the humble capacity of coal-hulks. Something in their appearance was familiar, and bringing a pair of binoculars to bear on them, I read the name " Cumbrae " on the bow of the longer one. The other bore no name, but the short hull with slanting stem and square stern convinced me that it was none other than the old " Balmoral." Old memories came crowding back on me: one of a lovely autumn evening fifteen years before, when I sailed in the " Cumbrae " from Fairlie round Inchmarnock, what time the harp and fiddle set the measure to the merry dancers on the fore-deck, and the well-nigh level rays of the setting sun reddened the glassy waters of the Sound of Bute ; another of a day still more remote, when I stood on the hurricane-deck of the " Balmoral," fascinated by the sight of the little crosshead, dancing up and down to the music of the riveters' hammers in the shipyards as she steamed up the river : pleasant old memories, that it did one's heart good to revive.

As the two lay there, shorn of everything above the bulwarks, the bright-coloured funnels, the burnished copper escape-pipes, the white-painted davits, the rails with their orderly rows of white lifebuoys, the daintily carved and gilded paddle-boxes, the varnished and brass-mounted deck-fittings; all gone: the bulwarks themselves broken and clumsily patched; nothing but the grimy black hulls remaining, albeit the graceful lines yet bore testimony to their old nobility; surrounded at high tide by unclean black water and at low by uncleaner black slime; a melancholy picture in dingy monochrome, save where the forces of decay, in decorative mood, had bedizened the bruised and battered plates with red patches of rust: one could not quite repress a feeling of resentment that, when their day of active service was over, their owners had not, in charity, spared them this degradation, by sending them to some shipbreaker, to be put decently out of existence.

" Dunoon Castle "

The " Dunoon Castle " was constructed by Messrs Wingate in 1867 as a protest on the part of the Dunoon and Rothesay carriers against what they considered the excessive rates which the steamboat companies were charging them. She was the last of the Clyde steamboats with the funnel behind the paddle-boxes, and the last to be fitted with a single steeple engine. The carriers' experience of steamboat-owning probably had the effect of modifying their opinion; it did not last long, and the steamer was put in the market and entered on a rather vagrant career. When I first recollect her she was running in company with the " Elaine," their funnels being black, with a white band over a red one, but I do not know to whom they belonged, or on what route they sailed. In 1875 the "Dunoon Castle" gravitated into the Sunday trade for Henry Sharp. A year or two later she came out with two funnels, both behind the paddles, and so she plied till 1883, when Messrs Hill & Co. bought her for the Fairlie and Millport service. This firm appear to have had a penchant for reclaiming Sunday-breakers; they had already rehabilitated the "Marquis of Lorne." When the "Dunoon Castle" appeared for them, her name had been changed to "Arran," and the extra funnel removed. Her last owners on the Clyde were Messrs Campbell & Gillies, who acquired her about 1885, and she sailed for them until they went out of business, when she was sold off the river. She is said to have found her way in succession to the Mersey, the Thames and the Shannon, a roundabout route which, no doubt, led eventually to the scrap-heap.

The Sunday boats half a century ago had a very bad reputation. Sabbatarianism was much stronger then than now, and the prejudice against the Sunday-breaker was such as to render her "taboo" on week-days also. Indeed, even in cases where a Sunday-breaker had changed hands and been wooed back to paths of respectability, the stricter section of the public continued to eye her askance, and her new owner was taught in practical fashion that the repentant sinner was not regarded with favour.

But apart from the Sabbatarian side of the question, there is no doubt that the clientele of the Sunday boats and the condition of things on board amply sufficed of themselves to justify their evil reputation. Most of the

"Arran," ex-"Dunoon Castle"

Photo by Messrs. J. Adamson & Son, Rothesay

VARIOUS BOATS

Sunday boats of the seventies and eighties belonged to Henry Sharp, a Gallowgate publican; the first two that I can remember were the "Petrel" and the "Kingstown." The Forbes-Mackenzie Act, which ordained the Sunday closing of public-houses, did not apply to the river-steamers, and the natural result was that the travellers by these boats were almost entirely "drouths," out to secure the alcoholic refreshment denied them ashore. The boats were simply floating "pubs." The "Petrel" sailed for Rothesay at half-past ten in the morning; the "Kingstown" to Greenock at half-past eight, returning in time to make a second trip, this time to Gourock, at half-past one. But their routes and destinations were matters of little moment; and it is probable that, when they arrived home, a large proportion of the passengers had no very definite idea as to where they had been.

"Petrel"

The "Petrel" was a rather larger edition of the "Balmoral," by the same builders, Barr & Macnab. She was one of three boats built in 1845 for the Glasgow and Greenock Railway Co., to run in connection with their trains, but the Railway Co. soon discarded the system of running their own boats. The "Petrel" plied in the Sunday service till 1874, but was afloat long after that, as her name appears in each issue of Lloyd's Register up to 1886, in which year the words "broken up" are added underneath.

"Kingstown"

The "Kingstown" was a freak. She was a short boat with two small funnels and deck-saloons fore and aft, and had a bow at either end, the sponsons being carried right round as in the case of the "Chancellor." She had more hull than that steamer, however, sufficient to form two small cabins below the main-deck. At the end of 1874 season the "Kingstown" was removed from the Clyde: she came back, however, many years later; some optimist having decided to give her a trial on the Broomielaw-Rothesay route, but as she occupied between six and seven hours on the passage, it is scarcely surprising that less than a week sufficed to finish the experiment.

The steamers I have mentioned in the foregoing pages comprise, so far as I can trace, all that were plying on the Firth of Clyde in 1872, whose voyagings did not extend farther than Campbeltown on the one hand, or Ayr on the other. Only one of these, the "Kintyre," was a screw-steamer. Most of the paddle-boats were flush-decked with a hurricane-deck over the engine-house, a type of vessel that has long since disappeared from the Firth. All had small side-houses built on the forward sponsons; one of these, usually the one on the port side, being fitted up as a galley, whose narrow funnel stuck up above the hurricane-deck just forward of the paddle-box, while the house on the starboard side contained lavatory arrangements of the primitive style then deemed adequate. The bulwarks of the after-deck were often surmounted by a canvas

VARIOUS BOATS

screen, serving to protect the passengers from spray, and at the same time to shut out the view of everything but the sky from anyone under middle height. The cabins, under the main-deck, entered usually from the after end, were stuffy little vaults with scant headroom, to which the light found its way partly through a few round ports near the water-line, and partly through a skylight on the main-deck. A demand for greater comfort sprang up among passengers in the eighties, and about that period a number of the flush-decked boats were fitted up with short deck-saloons—among the steamers thus altered were " Sultan," " Sultana," " Marquis of Bute," " Vivid," " Adela " and " Argyle."

The raised-quarterdeck boats, numbering some ten or a dozen, were a far more comfortable type than the flush-deckers. The last survivor of this class, the " Benmore," is not likely to see further service. In them, the after-deck from a few feet abaft of the engine-house was raised to the level of the main-rail. This arrangement secured a considerable increase of headroom and vastly improved the ventilation. Most of the earlier boats of this type had their cabins lit by a row of square windows set close together, admitting plenty of light, but the system probably had its drawbacks, as all the raised-quarterdeck boats after 1868 had the ordinary circular ports. The entrance to the cabin in all the boats of this class was at the break of the quarterdeck, under the stairway leading down from the hurricane-deck. An open rail, surrounding the raised deck, offered no obstruction to the view, and allowed even the tiniest tots to enjoy the fascination of watching the " soapy sapples " churned up by the paddle-wheel.

"Iona," "Dandie Dinmont," "Chancellor," "Kingstown" and "Bonnie Doon," of boats running regularly, and "Chevalier," an occasional visitor, had deck-saloons. None of these extended the full width of the vessel.

Few of the boats had navigating bridges, and the engine-room telegraph was a thing unknown; the skipper stood on the paddle-box and transmitted his orders to the engineer by means of a brass-headed knocker in the rail; three strokes for "Go ahead," two for "Back her," and one for "Stop her." There was no steam steering-gear; the hand-wheel, about as tall as an average man, stood on the hurricane-deck between the paddle-boxes, and just behind it was a low table, on which the steersman stood. So far as I can remember there were no steam-whistles then, but a warning bell was rung when small boats threatened to get in the way.

The engines of the period were fairly divided between the steeple, oscillating and diagonal types, although the last-mentioned was coming gradually into favour and superseding the other two. As a small boy, I had a strong preference for the steeple-engined boats. The engine-rooms of those days were completely boxed in, the windows being far above my low head, and if the engine were of diagonal or oscillating design, I could only hope to get an all too brief glimpse of it when raised in the parental arms. In a steeple-engined boat, the crosshead, bobbing up and down like a jack-in-the-box, was in full view and could be watched at leisure, independent of parental assistance.

Except, perhaps, in the Hutcheson boats of that

VARIOUS BOATS

time, not much was attempted in the way of uniform ; the skipper wore a brass-bound cap, but otherwise there was often nothing nautical about his attire. The deck hands usually had blue woollen jerseys with the steamer's name worked in red in front. In the engine-room, dongarees and an oil-can were the insignia of the profession. Some of the old-time skippers, such as Captain Barr of the Lochgoil boats, and Captain M'Lean of the " Marquis of Bute," eschewed even the nautical cap and wore square-topped felt hats ; M'Lean, indeed, had a white silk " tile " for special occasions. The captains of those days undertook the duties of purser besides attending to the navigation of the vessel. M'Lean, while performing either of these functions, never forgot that he was owner of the vessel as well, and the care he exercised to avoid any scraping of paint or gilt-work in taking a pier was only equalled by his diligence in inquiring the exact age of any child who seemed to be near the half-fare limit.

Of all these boats of 1872 but a few now remain, and these all belong to the MâcBrayne fleet. It is pleasant to reflect that, even in this utilitarian age, there are quarters where sentiment still lingers, and that owners can still be found who care to preserve old favourites like " Glengarry," " Mary Jane," " Iona," " Chevalier," and " Gael," so long after all their contemporaries have vanished into the limbo of the past.

PART II
ADDITIONS DURING THE PERIOD

The Broomielaw about 1876
with "Windsor Castle," "Balmoral" moored outside, thence, reading from the spectator, "Undine," "Vesta" and "Eagle." "Guinevere" and "Carrick Castle" on left.

CHAPTER VII

THE FIRST FIVE YEARS

THE years 1873 and 1874 were blank so far as the building of new boats for the Clyde service is concerned, and the tendency was rather to diminish than to augment the fleet, for during these two years the " Lorne," " The Lady Mary " and the " Heather Bell " were sent to other waters, the " Vulcan " sold out of the regular fleet and the " Venus " broken up. The " Kingstown " also left the Clyde about the end of the period.

In 1875 two steamers were built, one by Seath of Rutherglen and the other by Henderson of Partick.

" WINDSOR CASTLE "

The Rutherglen boat, the " Windsor Castle," was for the Lochgoil trade, and was slightly larger than her owners' former steamer, the " Carrick Castle." Like her, she had a diagonal engine by Wm. King & Co. Nearly all the Rutherglen productions of that period had fine scroll-work on bows and paddle-boxes, and the " Windsor Castle " was no exception. Her navigating bridge, placed forward of the funnel, anticipated the modern practice; it was a low erection, obstructing the passengers' view forward of the hurricane-deck. Originally the steamer was flush-decked, but after a couple of seasons, a deck-saloon was built abaft of the engine-house, a long erection, reaching nearly to the stern, but not extending the full width of the vessel. The " Windsor Castle " was maintained in the Lochgoilhead trade for a quarter of a century, and in 1900 was sent to Constantinople, where she is said to have been used as a ferry for conveying the ladies of the Sultan's harem across the harbour. Her name, which had not been changed, appears in a list of Turkish government vessels sold for breaking-up purposes about 1908.

" VICEROY "

The Henderson production was the " Viceroy," built for the Williamson fleet, and fitted with a diagonal engine about 20 per cent. more powerful than that of " Sultana." Rumour had it that she was intended for an improvement on that steamer, but so far as speed is concerned the new boat certainly had no chance against the old. Whether or not her speed was disappointing, the " Viceroy " proved herself a useful boat, and remained on the Firth for over thirty years, a period divided pretty equally between Williamson's and the South-Western Railway services. As launched, she was of raised-quarterdeck design, but shortly before the change of ownership, was converted into a saloon steamer. The saloon, however, was not placed on the quarterdeck, as in the case of the " Eagle " ; the greater portion of the raised deck was cut away to make room for it, and the floor of the saloon was on the level of the main-deck. About the same time the steamer was lengthened, and Lloyd's Register states that she was

"Viceroy"

Photo, by Messrs. J. Adamson & Son, Rothesay

"Benmore" leaving the Broomielaw
"Marquis of Bute" at quay

Photo, by Messrs. Valentine & Sons, Dundee

THE FIRST FIVE YEARS 61

fitted with a new boiler and engines, the latter of double diagonal design, much more powerful than her original single diagonal, but any increase of speed was not very marked. At the end of 1906 season, the " Viceroy " left the Clyde, to ply in southern waters, but I learn that she is no longer afloat.

The two steamers added to the fleet in 1876 both came from the Rutherglen yard, and both had the bow and paddle-boxes ornamented with scroll-work. Despite these additions, the number of steamers plying in this year had declined, as " Craigrownie," " Ardencaple," " Ardgowan " and " Levan " had ceased to run.

" Bonnie Doon " No. 2

The " Bonnie Doon," second of the name, and last of the Broomielaw-Ayr steamers, had a deck-saloon aft, of the same description as the one afterwards put into the " Windsor Castle." She resembled that steamer in general appearance, but was fully twenty feet longer. Though not particularly fast, she was a comfortable boat, but her engine, of diagonal pattern, by Campbell, had an unfortunate propensity for breaking down, which detracted from her efficiency. After the abandonment of the Ayr sailings in 1881, the " Bonnie Doon " took the place of the " Sheila " in the Campbell & Gillies fleet, but four years later she left the Clyde. She spent a season or two on Belfast Lough, and then went to the Bristol Channel, where the remainder of her days were passed. The shipbreakers got her shortly before the outbreak of war in 1914.

"Benmore"

The other steamer of 1876 was the "Benmore," which seems destined to go to the shipbreakers. Her adventures began early, for as she was being brought down the river from her builders to have her machinery put on board, she failed to negotiate the weir, and stuck upon it, lying there for some time, in imminent danger of breaking her back. However, she managed to get off all right and took her place on the noon run to Kilmun, which had previously been maintained by the "Vivid." During the season of 1876 the "Benmore" had the "Vesta" for her consort on the Holy Loch station, the "Vivid" being employed on odd excursions. The latter found her way back to the Kilmun trade the following year, when the "Vesta" joined the Gareloch boats. In 1884 all three steamers were bought by Captain Buchanan, under circumstances which will be referred to later. Two years afterwards Captain Buchanan had the "Benmore" altered, and during 1887 she plied on the Rothesay run with two funnels placed forward of the paddles. The change was not a success, as it brought the steamer considerably down by the head, and in the following year the one-funnelled arrangement was reverted to. She continued to ply for Captain Buchanan till 1892, passing then to Captain John Williamson, who employed her largely as a cargo boat, and had the scroll-work removed from her hull and paddle-boxes. A stranding inside the perch at Innellan once threatened to end her career, but either her staunchness or her luck stood her in good stead, and again she was rescued. During the war she

"Benmore" as she appeared in 1887

Photo, by an Amateur

THE FIRST FIVE YEARS 63

did good service in the Wemyss Bay trade, returning to the Williamson fleet after the Armistice. In October 1920 she was laid up for the season in the Harbour at Greenock, but her race was run. A fire breaking out on board did great damage, and in view of the high cost of materials and labour ruling at the time, her overhaul was put off until conditions should be more favourable. She is still lying in Greenock harbour, but is not likely to be again employed on the Clyde. Since the end of last century she had been the only example of the raised-quarterdeck class plying on the Firth; all the others had either been broken up, sold away, or transformed into saloon boats.

About a dozen years ago the " Benmore " had the unique experience of going amissing on the passage from Rothesay to Glasgow. Owing to a dense fog she was compelled to come to anchor off Dumbarton, and lay there for a couple of days, no word being obtainable of her whereabouts. Her few passengers, mostly of the hawker class, expressed themselves well pleased with the hospitality of the " Benmore," and showed great reluctance in leaving her when the Broomielaw was reached.

" Prince of Wales "

" Vessels for sale " in the newspapers of 31st July 1876 include " the iron paddle steamer ' Prince of Wales,' 61 tons register, all in thorough repair, having been recently overhauled, and now lying in D. & W. Henderson's slip at Partick." I have no recollection of this boat, but have traced her in Lloyd's Register as having been built by Reid of Port-Glasgow in 1845, and engined by Napier, and having been owned at Alloa for several years prior to the date of the advertisement. She is again advertised for sale on 22nd January 1877, this time " by virtue and in pursuance of an Order of Court," the upset price being fixed at £1200. During the summer of 1877 she plied to Garelochhead, and in the following year became a Sunday-breaker, taking up the " Kingstown's " old runs to Greenock and Gourock. She is not advertised after 1878.

Quite a revival of building took place in 1877, four steamers being put in the water, and three of these were exceptional boats. The South-Western Co. had set out to accelerate the service by Prince's Pier, and with the help of the " Sultana," were achieving considerable success. Passengers who travelled by the 4.5 express from St Enoch could reckon upon being landed in Rothesay as early as those who took the 4.10 from Bridge Street *via* Wemyss Bay, and the greater accessibility of the former station to the centre of the city procured for the Prince's Pier route the lion's share of the traffic. The Wemyss Bay Co., therefore, determined to accelerate their service also, and put on a very fast train at 4.35, carrying no luggage, and stopping only at Port-Glasgow for the collection of tickets.

" Sheila "

For the water transport, Messrs Campbell & Gillies ordered a fast steamer from Caird & Co., and that firm made no mistake. The " Sheila " was a raised-quarterdeck boat, much bigger than the " Sultana,"

THE FIRST FIVE YEARS

registering about a hundred tons more, and her diagonal engine was proportionately powerful. She certainly had her faults, but lack of speed was not one of them. The racing between these two boats during the seasons of 1877 and 1878 was the keenest that I can remember. Both steamers were ably sailed, the " Sultana " by Captain Alexander Williamson, and the " Sheila " by Captain Duncan Bell.

Let us fancy ourselves standing, at half-past five on a summer evening in 1877, alongside the then recently opened pier at Craigmore. Cast your eyes towards Wemyss Bay and you will see several small wreaths of smoke curling upward, marking where the steamers lie at the pier awaiting the arrival of the 4.35 express from Bridge Street. As we watch, the smoke-wreaths separate, and one of them is seen to be coming in our direction, while the small white speck from which it issues resolves itself gradually into the long white funnel of a steamboat. She grows rapidly larger as we watch, for she is travelling fast, and the dense smoke now curling from the funnel, together with the mass of white water that her wheels are throwing behind her, tells us that the " Sheila " is being driven. As she nears Toward Point the reason of her haste becomes apparent, for another smoke-wreath has appeared over Cowal, and a small black funnel comes in sight, moving rapidly past the low-lying land to the left of the lighthouse. The lighthouse buildings obscure it for a few seconds, and as it re-emerges, we recognise the graceful profile of the little " Sultana," travelling at her utmost speed, as she brings the passengers who have left St Enoch by the 4.5 express. The turn of her helm at

Toward buoy brings the two boats on parallel courses, and neck and neck they strain towards Craigmore. No change can be observed in their relative positions as we watch, but "Sheila" has an advantage in the porthand position, just sufficient, provided she can steam yard for yard with her opponent, to give her first turn of Craigmore pier. And so it comes about, and "Sultana," accepting the inevitable, is slowed up some five hundred yards off, lest the other's departure should find her too close to the pier, without steerage way.

The "Sheila" is brought alongside, mooring ropes are made fast fore and aft, the gangway is run across, and her passengers—not many, for there is as yet no great volume of traffic to Craigmore pier—step ashore. There is no particular hurry at this point, for here, it is evident, "Sultana" must perforce await her rival's convenience. At length the gangway is withdrawn, the forward mooring rope let go, and with the paddles reversing, the bow swings outward from the pier, as the strain comes on the after-hawser. As soon as the desired angle is reached, three strokes of the captain's knocker give the signal for "Full speed ahead," and the "Sheila" obeys slowly, for she is but an awkward starter, and the peculiar measure of her paddle-beats—four strokes and a pause, four strokes and a pause—proclaims that the whole staff of engine-room and stokehold are tailing on to the long starting-lever, to induce the obstinate crank to pass over the deadcentres. A heavy crank that! that sets the whole fabric of the vessel vibrating with each downward stroke, and makes the passengers, seated or standing

"Guy Mannering," ex-"Sheila"

Photo. by Messrs. J. Adamson & Son, Rothesay

THE FIRST FIVE YEARS

on the quarterdeck, sway back and forth in unison with its movement.

The stern of the "Sheila" has barely cleared the end of the quay ere the long, sharp stem of the "Sultana" is at the other end; her pilot knows his business, and her paddle-box grazes the piles as a backward turn of her wheels brings her up just at the right spot. A single mooring line is made fast aft, and while her few passengers are being hustled ashore, the ebb-tide is gently swinging her stem outward. The gangway is hurriedly hauled away, striking into the heels of the last passenger, and almost ere he has time to turn round and expostulate, the steamer is again under weigh, for, unlike her rival, she is sensitive to the starting-lever, and simply jumps off as the knocker goes.

We move a little way round the front, until Rothesay quay comes in sight. "Sheila" has secured the coveted berth at the western end, but a precious minute has been lost in mooring her, and as the first of her passengers step down the gangway, "Sultana" slips nimbly into the berth directly astern. With fewer passengers to disembark, she is ready to resume the race as soon as her rival; the paddle-wheels start revolving almost simultaneously, and the Rothesay clocks, striking six, find both steamers well clear of the quay, with "Sultana" this time in the inshore position, which "a spoke too far to port" by the other's pilot, cleverly turned to advantage by her own deft skipper, has enabled her to acquire. From where we stand, it is hard to tell how the race is going, but the white funnel swings round Ardbeg Point about a ship's length ahead of the black, and so they disappear behind the houses, leaving us to conjecture whether the one-length lead or the inshore position has proved the deciding factor in the finish at Port Bannatyne pier.

And so they raced, day after day, throughout the summers of 1877 and 1878, to the great delight of the spectators, most of them bigoted partisans of one or other boat, who lined the shore-roads round East and West Bays.

In her third season the " Sheila " had fallen off sadly in speed, and was no longer a match for her redoubtable little antagonist, nor did she recover until bought and overhauled by the North British Co., who placed her on the Craigendoran route under the name of " Guy Mannering." In their hands she re-established her reputation as a very fast boat, although to some extent overshadowed by her remarkable consort, the " Jeanie Deans." About 1890 considerable alterations were made in her appearance, the greater part of her raised quarterdeck being cut away and a deck-saloon fitted, while a small, detached deck-house, for use as a smoke-room, was erected on the fore-deck. She was sold out of the North British fleet in 1895, to make way for the " Redgauntlet," and thereafter, as the " Isle of Bute," bore Buchanan's house-flag in the up-river trade, the deck-house forward being replaced by a regular saloon. In her new occupation great speed was not regarded as a desideratum, and the old boat jogged leisurely between the Broomielaw and Rothesay for seventeen years, although on occasion, when called on, she could yet give proof that the fire of her youthful days was not altogether extinct. In May 1912 she was sold off the

THE FIRST FIVE YEARS 69

river to ply on the Lancashire coast, but as the last eight or nine issues of Lloyd's Register contain no mention of her, I am driven to conclude that the grand old " Sheila " must now be reckoned among the ships that were.

" Adela "

In the same year another steamer was built by Caird for the Wemyss Bay fleet, the " Adela," which replaced the " Lady Gertrude," and inherited the engine salved from that unfortunate vessel. A flush-decker, the last of the type to be built for the Clyde service, she was a commonplace boat alongside of the speedy " Sheila "; just a plain, substantial steamer, of very moderate speed, suited for all-the-year-round work in all sorts of weather. As built, she was very bluff in the bows, and broke a good deal of water to little purpose, but alterations were made forward which gave her a finer entrance. After she had been running for some years short saloons were placed on fore- and main-decks. She did yeoman service for Campbell & Gillies for about thirteen years, and when they went out of business, was sold to the south coast of England, where she bore the name of " Sea Breeze." Our last glimpse of her shows her plying as " La Corse " in Mediterranean waters.

" Glen Rosa " No. 1

Up to 1877 the ports on the eastern side of Arran were served by the " Guinevere " from the Broomielaw, and the " Rothesay Castle " from Ardrossan, but in that year two new steamers started running to the island. Between her morning up run from Rothesay and her evening down run, the "Sheila" sandwiched in a trip to Lamlash and back. Her sister-ship, the "Glen Rosa," also built by Caird, was started by her owners, Messrs Shearer of Gourock, in opposition to the "Guinevere" from the Broomielaw. In 1878 the old "Hero" was also placed on the station, and we had the absurd spectacle of three steamers leaving the Broomielaw for Lamlash every morning, all within half an hour. The "Hero's" sailing hour was 7.30, that of the "Glen Rosa" 7.45, and of the "Guinevere" 8 o'clock. Naturally this state of affairs could not last, as there was not nearly sufficient traffic for three boats. The "Hero" was the first to succumb, and she withdrew permanently from the Arran station at the end of 1878 season. A cut-throat competition went on between "Guinevere" and "Glen Rosa," and although the fares from Glasgow were not reduced, dwellers at the coast towns got the benefit of some very cheap excursions. Before the appearance of "Glen Rosa," the day return fare from Rothesay to Lamlash was two shillings, cabin, and eighteenpence, steerage. Gradually it was reduced, first to eighteenpence and one shilling, then to one shilling and ninepence, then ninepence and sixpence, but when "Guinevere" started accepting sixpence and fourpence, "Glen Rosa" did not follow suit. Circular excursions were advertised as a means of inducing traffic, Messrs Shearer coming to an arrangement with the Campbeltown Co., whereby passengers could travel to Lochranza by the "Gael," returning from Corrie by the "Glen Rosa," although evidently the journey between Lochranza and Corrie,

THE FIRST FIVE YEARS 71

about nine miles, had to be made at their own expense. On the "Guinevere" tickets were issued, entitling the holder to return by the "Rothesay Castle" *via* Ardrossan. Before the 1880 season commenced, however, the owners of "Guinevere" and "Glen Rosa" came to an arrangement, and the two boats sailed to Arran on alternate days, the steamer not so employed being run to Skipness, with a view to establishing a passenger trade to that village. The result of the Skipness venture was not encouraging, and the situation was relieved by the sale of the "Glen Rosa" to the Thames. There she created quite a sensation, attaining a speed of twenty-three miles an hour, no doubt with the assistance of current and tide. While on the Arran run she had been given little opportunity of showing her powers, the moderate "Guinevere" being quite unable to extend her. From the Thames the "Glen Rosa" found her way to the Bristol Channel, where she plied for many years for the Campbells; her appearance much altered, but her name unchanged. She went mine-sweeping during the war, but the experience was too severe for her constitution, and on her return she was condemned.

"Lord of the Isles" No. 1

But the most notable event in connection with the Clyde service in 1877 was the establishment of the daily service to Inveraray and back by the "Lord of the Isles." This was one of the most beautiful paddle steamers ever built; she sat like a duck in the water, and her whole design was a harmony without a single jarring note. Her launch took place from D. &. W. Henderson's yard at Partick on the 30th of May, and the scribes waxed enthusiastic over her steam-steering gear, her post-office on board, her superior lavatory arrangements, and her diagonal oscillating engine " of great power " which was expected to give her a speed of twenty statute miles an hour. A lock-out in the Clyde shipyards delayed her completion, and led to litigation between her owners and her builders, the former asking the Court to ordain that the builders should proceed with the work within forty-eight hours, or alternatively, give them access to their yard and plant, in order that they might have the steamer completed for themselves. The petition was refused, but fortunately there was not much further delay, and the " Lord of the Isles " took up her station on the 2nd of July. At first she only sailed from Greenock, with a call at Wemyss Bay, but after a few years her run was extended to Glasgow. Shortly after she began running, the Loch' Eck tour was established, passengers having the option of travelling either by the " Vivid " to Kilmun in connection with the 7.20 train from Bridge Street, or by the " Guinevere " to Dunoon in connection with the 9.5 from St Enoch. In the former case, they proceeded by coach to Inverchapel, thence by steamer " Fairy Queen " to the other end of Loch Eck, whence another coach conveyed them to Strachur. At Strachur they joined the " Lord of the Isles " on her way to Inveraray, and after spending an hour there, came home by her. Passengers going *via* Dunoon travelled thence to Loch Eck by coach, joined the " Fairy Queen " on her second trip, and reached Strachur in time to catch the " Lord of

"Lord of the Isles" No. 1

Phot. by Messrs. J. Adamson & Son, Rothesay

THE FIRST FIVE YEARS 73

the Isles" on her homeward journey. The enterprise of the Glasgow and Inveraray Steamboat Co., owners of the "Lord of the Isles," was deservedly rewarded, the various excursions enjoying great popularity.

The name of this steamer is associated with a distressing mishap that took place on the shores of Loch Fyne. In her early days big blasting operations were carried on at the granite quarries at Crarae and Furnace, and as the blasts were of a spectacular nature, excursions from Glasgow were arranged when they were about to take place. On one occasion a monster blast had been arranged at Crarae, and the "Lord of the Isles" took down a large number of excursionists to view the spectacle. The blast was carried out successfully, but a number of the excursionists, entering the quarry immediately afterwards, were overcome by gases which the explosion had liberated, and several of them succumbed.

In her first year the "Lord of the Isles" was commanded by Captain Robert Young, and he was succeeded by Captain M'Kinnon, who left her to become a tug-owner. Then Captain Downie came to her from the "Bonnie Doon," and remained by her till she left the Clyde, when he assumed command of her successor.

On the Thames, where she began to ply in 1891, the "Lord of the Isles" created a great sensation. The improvement in the standard of Thames river steamers dates from her advent there. While in the south her name was changed to "Jupiter," and alterations were made on her which quite destroyed the symmetry of her appearance. She was brought back to the Clyde about the beginning of the present century, as the "Lady of the Isles," for the Sunday traffic, but to those who had known her in her palmy days she was now a pitiable spectacle. She did no good after her return to the Clyde, and went to the scrap-heap at Dumbarton in 1904.

"Lough Foyle"

When the "Carrick Castle" made her appearance in 1870, her predecessor on the Lochgoilhead route, the "Loch Goil," a steeple-engined steamer with funnel aft, was transferred to Derry, where she plied as the "Lough Foyle." Under this name she reappeared on the Clyde in 1877, being engaged in the Gareloch trade. A few years later she was one of Henry Sharp's Sunday boats, and after a short spell there, joined the MacBrayne fleet. She sailed on the Caledonian Canal as the "Loch Ness" until broken up some fifteen years ago.

CHAPTER VIII

FROM THE "COLUMBA" TO THE OPENING OF THE GOUROCK ROUTE

THE advent of the "Lord of the Isles" was evidently regarded by Messrs MacBrayne, who had just succeeded Messrs Hutcheson, as a menace to their West Highland tourist trade, so to retain it, the "Columba" was ordered from Thomson, and she was launched from the Clydebank yard in the following year.

"COLUMBA"

The bold course was adopted of constructing her of steel, which was then in the experimental stage, as a material for shipbuilding, although an earlier steamer, called the "Windsor Castle," had plied on the Clyde for a single season nineteen years before. The "Columba" was, and is, a very notable steamer. In her, the general design of the "Iona" was followed, with the slanting bow and square stern, which were then already old-fashioned. It cannot be claimed for her that she presented the smart appearance of the "Lord of the Isles," but her internal appointments were well in advance even of that well-appointed steamer. Of course, she had all the latest gadgets, engine-room telegraphs, steam-steering gear and such, and she was fitted with a set of warping-sheaves, worked by steam, to facilitate handling her at piers. In her, deck saloons of the full width of the ship made their first appearance on the Clyde, giving room to have the settees placed thwartships with a spacious passage down the middle, in the style which has now become general. At the time of her building, the " Columba " was by far the biggest steamer in the service, and although there are now one or two which exceed her in tonnage, her length of over three hundred feet has not been equalled. Her name is a household word to the tourist, representing all that is best in accommodation and catering. After forty-four years' service she still travels fast, and she bids fair to outlive most of her human contemporaries.

" Brodick Castle "

The " Brodick Castle," another production of 1878, was built by H. M'Intyre & Co., to the order of Captain Buchanan, and was fitted with the original double diagonal engine of the " Eagle." She was rather of hybrid appearance, with two funnels forward of the paddles, a big topgallant forecastle, and a saloon with alleyways alongside, extending about halfway aft from the engine-house, aft of which the quarter-deck was raised to the level of the main-rail. She sailed on the Ardrossan-Arran station during the summer of 1878; the winter service—which, by the way, was only on three days of the week—being taken by the " Rothesay Castle." The latter being thereafter sent abroad, the " Brodick Castle " sailed winter and summer till 1886, when she was sold off the river. For many years she plied under her original name at Bournemouth.

"Brodick Castle"

Photo. by Messrs. G. W. Wilson & Co., Aberdeen (now Mr. Fred. W. Hardie)

"Edinburgh Castle"

Photo. by an Amateur

"KINLOCH"

The screw steamer "Kinloch" for the Campbeltown Co. came out in the same year as the "Columba" and "Brodick Castle." A. & J. Inglis were her builders. While not quite so graceful in her lines as the yacht-like "Kintyre," she is a very beautiful model. The clipper bow retained by the Campbeltown Co. imparts to their vessels an elegance that is seldom found in modern steamers. The "Kinloch" still plies for her original owners in the trade for which she was built.

"EDINBURGH CASTLE"

The fleet underwent a reduction in 1879, the "Undine," "Rothesay Castle" and "Prince of Wales" disappearing, while only one new steamer, the "Edinburgh Castle," for the Lochgoil trade, was added. R. Duncan & Co., of Port-Glasgow, were the builders of the hull, Rankin & Blackmore supplying the diagonal engine. The principal feature about this boat was her enormous paddle-wheels, measuring twenty-two feet across, which, however, were not found very satisfactory. The height of the centres tended to topheaviness, while the paddle-shafts, far above the level of the main-deck, formed awkward obstructions in the alleyways alongside the engine-house. The huge paddle-boxes were a blemish on her appearance, giving her a short, hump-backed look. This steamer had a deck saloon abaft the engine-house, similar to those of "Windsor Castle" and "Bonnie Doon." Her whole lifetime was spent on the Lochgoilhead run, and she was broken up at the end of 1913. She was then thirty-four years old, not a great age for a Clyde steamer, but perhaps lack of funds had interfered with her proper upkeep.

"IVANHOE"

In 1880 the experiment was tried of running a steamer on teetotal lines : no alcoholic liquor to be sold on board. The Frith of Clyde Steam Packet Co. was formed with this object, Captain James Williamson being appointed managing director and skipper, and the "Ivanhoe" was laid down at Meadowside. In design both of hull and machinery she closely resembled the "Lord of the Isles," although smaller, but she never conveyed quite the same impression of buoyancy. In appointments and upkeep she was more like a yacht than a steamer for commercial purposes, her decks were always kept scrubbed to a snowy whiteness, gold braid was much in evidence both on the bridge and in the engine-room, and the deck-hands were attired, yachtsman fashion, in white blouses with navy blue collars. These attractions met with public appreciation, the vessel's one drawback could be discounted by a little forethought before embarking, and the "Ivanhoe flask" of capacity suitable for a day's outing, is said to have found a ready sale in Glasgow. The steamer's starting-point was Helensburgh, thence the route lay by way of Prince's Pier, Dunoon and Rothesay, through the Kyles of Bute to Arran, returning *via* the Garroch Head. On Saturdays excursions were made round Ailsa Craig. The "Ivanhoe" remained on this station about fourteen years, going to the Manchester Canal

"Ivanhoe"

Photo. by Messrs. J. Adamson & Son, Rothesay

when it was opened. She did not remain long there, and on her return joined the fleet of the Caledonian Steam Packet Co. An addition made to her equipment may or may not be regarded as an improvement. Bars were fitted in the lower saloons, fore and aft, although an inscription on the silver-plated water-fountain in the main saloon still continued to admonish the traveller that he might "gang faur'er an' fare waur." After some fifteen years in the Caledonian service, the "Ivanhoe" was sold for the up-river traffic, eventually coming into the hands of Captain John Williamson. During the war she did good service on the Firth for the Caledonian Co. She ceased plying at the end of 1919 season, and after lying for the greater part of a year in Greenock harbour, was towed to Dumbarton to be broken up.

"Scotia"

Captain Duncan Stewart retired from the steamboat business at the end of August 1879, and his one remaining steamer, the "Elaine," was transferred to Captain Buchanan. The Buchanan advertisement of 1st September contains the names of "Eagle," "Elaine," and new saloon steamer "Scotia" (building). The new boat was launched by M'Intyre in the following spring. A double steeple engine, the last of the steeple type, was fitted by Wm. King & Co. The "Scotia" had two funnels placed fore and aft, but otherwise bore a good deal of resemblance to the "Brodick Castle," although her saloon was of full width, and she had originally no forecastle. After five seasons running between Glasgow and Rothesay she went on the Broomielaw-Arran route in succession to the "Guinevere," and two years later she was provided with a forecastle, and took the place of the " Brodick Castle " on the Ardrossan-Arran station. The South-Western Co. bought her in 1891, to run on their own account, but in the following year she was superseded by the " Glen Sannox," and in the summer of 1893 was sold and sent to the Bristol Channel.

"CHANCELLOR" No. 3

A new " Chancellor," built of steel by Chambers of Dumbarton, and having a double diagonal engine by M. Paul & Co., replaced the old steamer of the name on the Arrochar route in 1880. She was the last to have the old-fashioned, narrow saloons, with alleyways all round. Changing owners she continued to trade to Arrochar for the Lochgoil Co., but in 1891 was purchased by the South-Western Railway Co. They employed her chiefly between Prince's Pier and the lochs, until she was sold out of their fleet and sent to Ferrol. She plied there for a number of years as the "Comercio" before being converted into a barge.

"MINARD CASTLE"

In 1881 no new steamers were built, and the fleet was reduced by the departure of the "Carrick Castle," "Vale of Clwyd" and "Glen Rosa," while the solitary addition of the following year was the screw-steamer "Minard Castle." Built by Fullerton of Paisley for the goods and passenger trade between Glasgow and Inveraray, this graceful little steamer is a miniature of the best Channel steamers of her time. Some years ago her appearance was much impaired by the removal of her masts, to enable her to berth above Glasgow Bridge, but these have since been restored, and she presents a very favourable contrast to the other cargo steamers on the Firth, whose designs, for the most part, are strictly utilitarian.

In 1882 the North British Steam Packet Co., which for many years had traded no farther south than Dunoon, inaugurated an infrequent service to Rothesay with the "Sheila," which they had purchased from Campbell & Gillies.

"Meg Merrilies"

In the following year Craigendoran pier was opened, and the North British Co. went much more vigorously into the Rothesay trade, getting the "Meg Merrilies" from Messrs Barclay, Curle & Co. to run as a consort to the "Sheila," now re-named "Guy Mannering." The "Meg" had two funnels forward of the paddle-boxes, and a deck saloon aft, and was propelled by a pair of diagonals. Unfortunately, her speed failed to realise expectations, with the result that, after running for a season, she was returned to her builders. The following year found her on Belfast Lough, but in 1885 she came back to the Clyde for Campbell's Kilmun trade. As the result of an accident, the "Meg" had to be re-boilered, and reappeared with only one funnel. She was one of the first steamers acquired by the Caledonian Steam Packet Co., and her service with them lasted till 1901. She plied as the "Maua" in the harbour of Rio de Janeiro, but has disappeared from the last issue of Lloyd's Register.

The "Meg Merrilies" was the last steamer built entirely of iron for the Clyde service. Her two immediate successors in the North British fleet were constructed partly of iron and partly of steel, but all later boats have been of steel.

"JEANIE DEANS"

To replace the "Meg" in the North British fleet, the "Jeanie Deans" was built by Barclay, Curle & Co. in 1884. She closely resembled the "Guy Mannering" in design of hull and engines, and was the last to be built of raised-quarterdeck type. Her performances quite atoned for the shortcomings of the "Meg Merrilies," and for several years she was unquestionably the fastest boat on the Firth. The extra distance from Craigendoran was a handicap to the North British Co. in competition with the Wemyss Bay and Prince's Pier routes, and only the possession of two such fast boats as the "Jeanie Deans" and the "Guy Mannering" enabled them to secure some share of the Rothesay traffic. In 1894 the "Jeanie Deans" was equipped with decksaloons to bring her up to date. Alterations on the original design of a steamer are seldom an unqualified success, and her case was no exception, for both speed and stability were impaired. In 1896 she left the Clyde, to run between Derry and Moville, but two years later came back for the Sunday trade, her name being changed to "Duchess of York." Proving un-

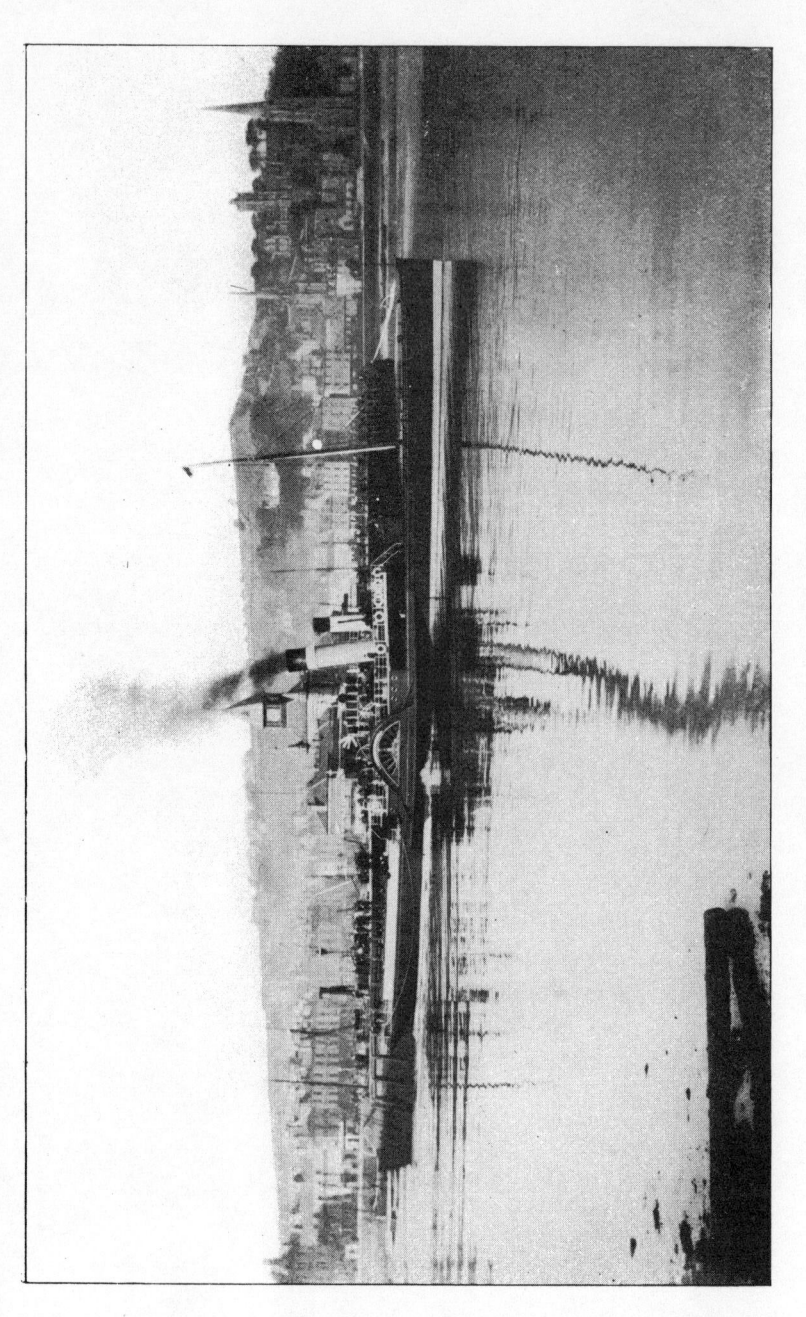

"Jeanie Deans" leaving Rothesay
"Adela" at quay, "Athole" in dock.

Photo. by Messrs. Poulton (now Messrs. W. Ritchie & Sons)

successful, she lay in Bowling harbour for more than one season, ere Captain Buchanan bought her and placed her on the Broomielaw-Rothesay route as the " Isle of Cumbrae." During the war she was employed in the South-Western service, and this was followed by a spell in Greenock harbour, whence she was taken to Dumbarton quite recently for breaking-up.

The " Cluthas "

The " Cluthas," for passenger traffic in Glasgow harbour, were started in 1884, but their history is quite distinct from that of the ordinary river-steamers, and will be dealt with separately.

" Diana Vernon "

The next North British addition was the " Diana Vernon," also by Barclay, Curle & Co., launched in 1885. This was a small saloon steamer, not quite in the first rank for speed, but her handiness at piers more than compensated for this, for she steered like a witch. Like many another handy boat, she was tender, so tender, in fact, that no passengers were carried on the top of the fore-saloon, the upper deck being railed off just forward of the funnel. The " Diana " sailed on the Holy Loch and Gareloch routes for eight seasons, and after twenty years in the south of England as the " Worthing Belle," went to Constantinople, where she was re-named " Touzla."

"Davaar"

The "Davaar," launched by the London and Glasgow Shipbuilding and Engineering Co., has the clipper bow and graceful lines that distinguish all the screw-steamers of the Campbeltown Co. She is considerably larger than the "Kinloch" or "Kintyre," and her passenger accommodation is superior. As built, she had two tall funnels close together, but after a number of years these were removed, and a single funnel substituted, one of the few instances where a vessel's appearance has been improved by alterations on the original design.

In her early days her career was nearly cut short by a stranding on Davaar Island, but fortunately it was found possible to re-float her. In spite of turbine opposition, the "Davaar" and "Kinloch" still contrive to carry on a remunerative all-the-year-round trade.

"Grenadier"

Of 1885 also was the "Grenadier," a two-funnelled, clipper-bowed paddle steamer, which took her place in the MacBrayne fleet. Her builders, Messrs Thomson, fitted her with a compound oscillating engine, the first compound engine in the river-fleet, and the only one of its type. The "Grenadier's" Clyde sailings are confined to the winter months; in summer her head-quarters are at Oban. She was requisitioned for mine-sweeping during the war, but has survived to resume her former occupation.

In 1884 Captain Bob Campbell's affairs were not flourishing, and towards the end of that year his two steamers, "Benmore" and "Vivid," were sold to Captain Buchanan, who retained the former in the Kilmun trade. Captain Campbell, however, obtained some backing, which enabled him to buy the "Meg Merrilies," and run her in opposition. Her hour of sailing from the Broomielaw was noon, the "Benmore" leaving five minutes earlier. Both steamers wore the all-white funnel associated with the Holy Loch route, and as usual in cases of keen competition, the public got the benefit of cheap fares. The steerage return by the "Meg" was one shilling, and by the "Benmore" ninepence. Captain Campbell's long connection with the Kilmun trade secured him a popularity that won the day, and after a single season the "Benmore" was withdrawn.

"Waverley" No. 2

As a consort to the "Meg," Captain Campbell had the "Waverley" built by M'Intyre. She was a one-funnelled boat, similar in dimensions to the "Meg," but for some reason or other seems to have been found unsuitable for the trade. In her second year she ran excursions to Ayr, going afterwards to the Bristol Channel and becoming the pioneer of the splendid fleet now plying on that estuary for the Campbells. The "Waverley" had a long life on the Bristol Channel, and was mine-sweeping during the war, but on her return from that occupation, was found to be fit only for breaking-up.

"Madge Wildfire"

When the "Waverley" was transferred to the Ayr run in 1886, her place on the Kilmun station was taken by a new steamer, the "Madge Wildfire," built at Ayr by Messrs M'Knight & Co. She was smaller than the "Waverley," but similar in design, having a deck saloon abaft the engine-house. The "Meg" and "Madge" were bought by the Caledonian Steam Packet Co. in 1888, and took their places on the Gourock route when it was opened in the following year. That company evidently found the "Madge" a useful boat, for they kept her for nearly twenty years, and went to great expense in compounding her engine and fitting her with a boiler of modern type in place of her old-fashioned haystack. When sold out of their fleet, she sailed for a season or two in the Broomielaw-Rothesay trade for a Dumbarton firm. Later she became the "Isle of Skye" in the Buchanan fleet, and on war service was employed as a tender to the fleet at Invergordon.

"Victoria"

The "Victoria," the last boat to be built for the Campbell & Gillies Wemyss Bay fleet, came from Blackwood & Gordon's yard in 1886. She was a two-funnelled boat, of dimensions about the same as those of the "Ivanhoe," and although by no means so well-finished as that steamer, was a commodious and comfortable boat. With a powerful double diagonal engine she attained considerable speed. She was the first of the Clyde steamers to be fitted with electric light, but

"Victoria"

Photo. by Messrs. J. Adamson & Son, Rothesay

"Lucy Ashton"

Photo, by the Author

TO OPENING OF GOUROCK ROUTE

this gave a good deal of trouble, as the system had not then been brought to its present perfection. After her owners' retiral in 1890, the "Victoria" entered upon a varied career. A season on Belfast Lough, and another on excursions from the Broomielaw, and a short period on the Thames, were followed by a return to her native waters for the Sunday trade. A fire on board at the Broomielaw, which did great damage, terminated her career in home waters, and her name drops out of Lloyd's Register, but she is said to have been patched up and sent to Bermuda.

"Seagull"

During the Glasgow Fair holidays in 1886, a Shields tug called the "Seagull" maintained the Innellan and Toward connections of the Wemyss Bay Co., releasing the regular boats for excursions to ports more favoured by the holiday-makers. The "Seagull" only ran for a week, but even on this ferry service her lack of adequate passenger accommodation caused a good deal of resentment.

"Lucy Ashton"

After a blank year, the "Lucy Ashton" came from Rutherglen in 1888, to ply between Craigendoran and the Holy Loch, in succession to the old "Dandie Dinmont." With nothing striking about her, she has evidently given satisfaction to her owners, who have not spared money to bring her up to date. After she had run some fourteen years, they re-engined her, a compound diagonal by A. & J. Inglis replacing the original diagonal with which Hutson & Corbet had fitted her, and a year or two later her saloons were entirely reconstructed. She now runs on the Gareloch, and also maintains the Greenock and Helensburgh ferry service.

"Fusilier"

The "Fusilier" launched by Messrs D. M'Arthur & Co. in the same year for Messrs MacBrayne scarcely belongs to the Clyde fleet, most of her sailing having been done from Oban, but while the war lasted was running in the Wemyss Bay service. She is clipper-bowed like the "Grenadier," but her engine, by Hutson & Corbet, is of old-fashioned, non-compound diagonal type.

CHAPTER IX

FROM THE OPENING OF THE GOUROCK ROUTE TO THE COMING OF THE TURBINE

1889 saw the opening of Gourock railway and pier. Two new steamers had been built, and these, along with the bought-in "Madge Wildfire" and "Meg Merrilies," took their places on the route at its commencement. The new boats were the first to have compound diagonal engines.

"CALEDONIA"

The "Caledonia," which came from the yard of J. Reid & Co. at Port-Glasgow, had the two cylinders placed tandem, to operate a single crank. This form of engine was afterwards applied to other three steamers belonging to the Caledonian Co., but it did not find favour with other owners. The "Caledonia" was a moderate-sized steamer, with full deck-saloons fore and aft, elegantly fitted up for passengers, and on her bridge were telegraphs communicating not only with the engine-room, but with the men at the mooring-lines. She is still in the Caledonian fleet, although a collision on a French river when on Government service nearly brought her to an untimely end.

"Galatea"

The "Galatea," built and engined by Caird, was a much bigger steamer, with two funnels, and her engine was a two-crank, compound diagonal, the design that has been adopted in nearly all modern paddle boats. It was very powerful, too powerful indeed for the rather fragile hull, so that it was found undesirable to drive her. She was to the full as well appointed as the "Caledonia," and established herself as a popular favourite on the Firth. The "Galatea" was expatriated from the Clyde in 1906, to ply in Mediterranean waters, and the absence of her name from Lloyd's Register may indicate that she is no longer to the fore.

"Marchioness of Breadalbane" and "Marchioness of Bute"

In the year following the Gourock opening, the Caledonian Co. extended its range of action, taking over the Wemyss Bay service from Campbell & Gillies. The Wemyss Bay trains which, up till then, had made Bridge Street station their terminus, were now run right into the Central. The Caledonian fleet had been increased by the addition of the "Marchioness of Breadalbane" and "Marchioness of Bute," practically sister-ships to the "Caledonia"; the only noticeable difference being that their navigating bridges were placed forward of the funnels, whereas the earlier boat had hers between the paddle-boxes. The "Marchioness of Bute" went to the Tay about fifteen years ago. Both steamers were requisitioned for mine-sweeping

"Galatea"

Photo. by the Author

"Duchess of Hamilton"

Photo, by Messrs. J. Adamson & Son, Rothesay

and both survived. The "Breadalbane" now maintains the Wemyss Bay connection to Largs and Millport.

"Duchess of Hamilton"

An important addition to the railway services took place in 1890, when the Lanarkshire and Ayrshire Railway was opened, affording the Caledonian Co. an outlet at Ardrossan for the Arran trade, for which a magnificent steamer, called the "Duchess of Hamilton," was built by Messrs William Denny & Bros. at Dumbarton. This proved to be one of the most successful boats ever seen on the Firth. Her immense saloon, thirty feet in width, was sumptuously furnished; her promenade deck extended the full length and width of the vessel, and the symmetry and balance of her whole design rendered her a joy to look upon. Her popularity was at once assured, and her superiority over the old "Scotia" secured for the new route the major portion of the Arran traffic. When the turbine steamer, "Duchess of Argyll," appeared on the Arran route in 1906, the "Duchess of Hamilton" was placed in the excursion trade from Gourock, for which she proved herself admirably adapted. Taken into Government service during the war, she was lost by striking a mine in the English Channel.

"Argyll"

A little screw-steamer called the "Argyll" was placed in the Fairlie-Campbeltown trade about 1890. Built by Messrs R. Duncan & Co. in 1885, with compound engines by Messrs Muir & Houston, she had but a short career, being wrecked in Loch Ryan in 1893.

" Cygnus "

It was about the beginning of the nineties that the old " Inveraray Castle " retired from active service, and to replace her, Messrs MacBrayne bought in an old paddle-steamer called the " Cygnus," which had come from Henderson's yard at Renfrew in 1854, two-masted with bowsprit and fiddle-head and two tall funnels abaft the paddles. In her second season on the Inveraray route she had become the "Brigadier," having been re-engined and boilered. The two funnels had been replaced by a single one, the fiddle-head had made way for a finely-carved figurehead in military costume, and a liberal application of gilding and red paint had quite transformed her appearance. Transferred not long afterwards to the Hebridean trade, she was put ashore and wrecked on a northern coast.

1891 brought one addition to the Caledonian and two to the North British fleets, while a new " Lord of the Isles " replaced the original steamer of the name on the Inveraray route.

" Marchioness of Lorne "

The " Marchioness of Lorne," built by Russell & Co. of Port-Glasgow for the Caledonian Co., was intended principally for the winter trade to Arran. As in the case of the " Duchess of Hamilton," her promenade deck was carried right forward to the bow. The engines, by Rankin & Blackmore, were the first on the triple-expansion principle to be placed in a Clyde riverboat. There were but two cranks, one operated by the low-pressure cylinder and the other by the high and intermediate, placed tandem fashion. The innovation does not appear to have been immediately successful, as the compound engine reappeared in the Company's next steamer, but in two later boats, built during the present century, the triple-expansion principle has been reverted to. The "Marchioness of Lorne" is a short steamer of considerable beam, and was not designed to be fast. Since her return from war service she has not been re-conditioned, and now presents rather a sorry appearance as she lies in Bowling harbour.

"Lady Clare" and "Lady Rowena"

The North British steamers, "Lady Clare" and "Lady Rowena," were built respectively by D. M'Arthur & Co., and M'Knight of Ayr. Both had non-compound single diagonal engines by Hutson & Corbet. The "Lady Clare" was principally employed in the Gareloch trade, while the "Lady Rowena" succeeded the "Chancellor" on the Arrochar route. Neither of these boats had any lower saloon abaft the engine-house, but in the "Lady Rowena" the saloon on the foredeck extended forward of the mast and the full width of the ship, and formed a commodious dining-room. The "Lady Clare" went to Lough Foyle nearly twenty years ago, and except for an interlude of mine-sweeping, has been plying there ever since. The "Lady Rowena's" career was rather a varied one. Sold foreign about the end of last century, she returned to the Clyde and ran for a couple of seasons on the Broomielaw-Rothesay station, before going on war service. After her return to civilian life she was sold and re-sold, and finally went to a shipbreaker at the modest price of £450.

"Lord of the Isles" No. 2

The second "Lord of the Isles" was by the same builders as her predecessor, and similarly engined. Captain Downie, of the older boat, took command of her, and remained in charge so long as she was on the Inveraray route. The new boat was rather larger than the old, and although her appearance suffers by comparison, is not without her share of good looks. After she had been sailing for some years, her promenade deck, which reached at first only to the mast, was extended to the bow, giving increased accommodation. For a number of years she plied on the Inveraray route, with success, but the opposition started by the boats of the Turbine Co. took away her trade, and in 1912 that firm bought her up, employing her mainly on excursions from the Broomielaw round the Island of Bute. The "Lord of the Isles" had the good fortune not to be requisitioned for war work, and was for several years a very useful factor in maintaining connections with the ports on the upper Firth above the boom at Dunoon. Her present owners have retained the old Lochgoil funnel, with which her name has always been associated.

"Lord of the Isles" No. 2

Photo, by the Author

"Herald"

In the same year that the second "Lord of the Isles" was built there came back to the Clyde for the Fairlie-Campbeltown trade a steamer called the "Herald," which had plied to Campbeltown when she was built by Caird, a quarter of a century before. I do not think she ran for more than a single season after her reappearance. Some years later I saw her in the Pudzeoch at Renfrew, where, probably, she was broken up.

The South-Western Railway Co., alarmed at the inroads which the Caledonian Co. were making on their coast trade by means of the new Gourock and Ardrossan routes, applied for, and obtained parliamentary powers to own steamers, and set about improving their service. Big improvements were made at Prince's Pier, and the nucleus of a fleet was secured by the buying up of the four Williamson steamers, the "Viceroy," "Sultana," "Sultan" and "Marquis of Bute," besides the "Chancellor" and the "Scotia." These purchases took place in the autumn of 1891, and at the same time three powerful new steamers were laid down, two for the traffic on the upper Firth, and one to replace the "Scotia" on the Ardrossan-Arran station, in opposition to the "Duchess of Hamilton."

"Neptune" and "Mercury"

The first two, the "Neptune" and "Mercury," by Napier, Shanks & Bell, were bigger and faster than the Caledonian boats to which they were opposed, and by their means the South-Western Co. were able to secure their share of the passenger traffic.

After nearly a quarter of a century of service, both were requisitioned for war work, and both came in contact with mines. The "Neptune's" mishap occurred off Gravelines, and she was blown to pieces, with eighteen of her crew, but the "Mercury" had better fortune. She struck a mine off the East Coast, and had her stern blown off, but managed to keep afloat, and reached port, where the damage was repaired. She was only at sea for a single day before striking another mine; this time it was the bow that was blown off, two lives being lost; but again she was salved, surviving to rejoin the South-Western fleet after the Armistice.

"Glen Sannox"

The third steamer, the "Glen Sannox," built and engined by Messrs J. & G. Thomson, was some ten feet longer than the "Duchess of Hamilton," and furnished in equally lavish manner. Her engines were of the same type as those of the "Duchess," but more powerful, and she was a faster boat. Her side-plating, from the bow to the forward end of the saloon, was carried right up to the promenade deck, and with her two smartly-raked funnels, she presented a very imposing appearance. With two such boats as the "Duchess of Hamilton" and "Glen Sannox" in active opposition, Arran enjoyed for several years an excellent service, such as it had never known before, the time from Glasgow to Brodick being cut down to eighty-five minutes; but it did not last, the companies coming to an arrangement, as a

"Mercury"

Photo. by the Author

"Glen Sannox"

Photo. by Messrs. Maclure, Macdonald & Co., Glasgow

result of which, Arran is now very little better catered for than in the old days of the "Scotia" and "Brodick Castle." The war experience of the "Glen Sannox" was brief, as she was shortly returned as unsuitable, and resumed her place on the Arran station. Even then she was not free from the danger of mines, and on several occasions her sailings were cancelled, and only resumed after sweeping operations had guaranteed a measure of security.

By agreement between the companies, the "Glen Sannox" now maintains the Arran sailings in connection with both railways.

"Isle of Arran"

A contemporary of these boats is the "Isle of Arran," of the Buchanan fleet, the last Rutherglen production for the river service. Her first few seasons were spent on the Broomielaw-Arran route, but that service was withdrawn and the boat placed on the Rothesay run. Afternoon excursions from that port were started, the course being round Cumbrae and to Loch Striven on alternate days. The fares were a marvel of cheapness; the passengers could board the steamer at Glasgow at eleven in the forenoon, and sail continuously till eight o'clock, enjoying a good dinner and plain tea, all for a payment of four shillings and sixpence. Of course, with the advance of prices that has taken place within the last few years, such bargains are no longer possible, but even with the fare almost doubled, the excursions must surely rank among the cheapest in existence. The steamer, although not fast, is comfortably, though not extravagantly furnished, and the catering is well done. The " Isle of Arran " was mine-sweeping during the war, and so far as I know, her operations were not fraught with misadventure. On re-conditioning, she had her navigating bridge shifted forward of the funnel, a change which several of the boats underwent on their return from war service. She still does useful work from the Broomielaw.

"Minerva" and "Glen Rosa" No. 2

The " Minerva " and " Glen Rosa " were added to the South-Western fleet in 1893. These boats were built at Clydebank, and were smaller than the " Neptune " and " Mercury," with engines of the same type and of proportionate power. They were able, handy little vessels of slightly greater draught than the usual run of Clyde coast-boats, being intended for all-the-year-round work. From the bow to the forward end of the saloon they were decked over at the level of the rail, a sort of monkey-forecastle being thus formed, which was surmounted by an open rail, and which must have been rather an uncomfortable spot when plunging into a head sea between Ardrossan and Brodick in winter-time. These two steamers served on the Firth till the war. They survived their work among the mines, but the " Minerva " did not return to her native waters, being taken over permanently by Government. The " Glen Rosa," however, was re-conditioned, and resumed her place on the Firth.

In 1894 there was a lull in building. Although

"Isle of Arran"

Photo. by the Author

"Culzean Castle"

Photo. by Messrs. Maclure, Macdonald & Co., Glasgow

TO THE COMING OF THE TURBINE 99

thirteen new steamers had been added to the fleet since the end of the eighties, its numbers had not increased, as the withdrawals had been quite as numerous. These included the five steamers of the old Wemyss Bay fleet, the " Victoria," " Adela," " Lancelot," " Argyle " and " Arran," the North British steamers " Gareloch " and " Diana Vernon," the ill-fated " Guinevere," the " Scotia," the " Balmoral," the " Cumbrae," and three boats which had gone to the Manchester Canal, the " Eagle," " Shandon " and " Ivanhoe."

" Culzean Castle "

A stranger found her way to the Clyde about this period, the " Culzean Castle," launched in 1891 as the " Windsor Castle " by the Southampton Shipbuilding and Engineering Co. for service in the south of England. This steamer had the only three-crank engine that has appeared in the Clyde service; it was on the triple-expansion system. She was clipper-bowed, with two masts and a very big funnel of elliptical shape, and was a commodious, powerful and weatherly boat, but the frequency with which she persisted in breaking down discounted these qualities. Her first service on the Clyde was on the Campbeltown run, but after a season or two she was re-named " Carrick Castle," and transferred to excursion work on the upper Firth. This did not last long, and she went abroad, and is now in Japan, bearing the name of " Tenri Maru," her third since leaving the Clyde, and her sixth altogether, so that one is inclined to fear that her defect has not yet been completely overcome. If so, it is a pity, as in all other respects she is a particularly fine ship.

The Caledonian Co. added one, and the North British Co. two steamers to their fleets in 1895.

"DUCHESS OF ROTHESAY"

The "Duchess of Rothesay" for the former company is a Clydebank boat, compound-engined, a smaller boat than the "Duchess of Hamilton," but something like her in general design. She was placed on the Arran service from Gourock in succession to the "Ivanhoe," and plied there for a time, in addition to maintaining railway connections on the upper Firth. Her war experiences included, besides the destruction of a great number of mines, the towing into an East Coast port of the wreck of a Zeppelin, which had fallen into the North Sea. The "Duchess of Rothesay" kept afloat throughout the war, only to be sunk at her moorings while being re-conditioned, a sea-cock having been inadvertently left open. She lay submerged for some weeks, with nothing but the upper portion of the funnel showing above water, before being raised and re-furbished.

"REDGAUNTLET"

The "Redgauntlet" for the North British Co. came from Barclay, Curle's Scotstoun yard, and, like the earlier steamers of this company, was propelled by a single diagonal engine of non-compound type. She replaced the "Guy Mannering" on the Rothesay route,

"Duchess of Rothesay"

Photo, by the Author

"Dandie Dinmont" No. 2

Photo, by the Author

where she ran with success for some years. After the appearance of the "Kenilworth," the "Redgauntlet" ran on excursions from Craigendoran round Arran. While thus employed she was put ashore near Sliddery in August 1899, and remained fast, her passengers being taken off in carts. For a time it looked as if the steamer was to become a wreck, but she was eventually got off and repaired, plying on the Clyde for some nine years longer, before being sent to the Firth of Forth.

"Dandie Dinmont" No. 2

The "Dandie Dinmont" for the same owners was built and engined by A. & J. Inglis. Her engines were of the same kind as those of the "Redgauntlet," but less powerful, and she was a smaller boat. She was designed principally for the Dunoon and Holy Loch traffic, and not being requisitioned by Government, remained in it during the war. An addition of fourteen feet to her length has added to her efficiency.

"Glenmore"

As a consort to the "Benmore," the "Glenmore" was built by Russell & Co., Port-Glasgow, for Captain John Williamson. She was a small steamer with a compound engine, up-to-date and economical, though not fast. Her lifetime on the Clyde only extended to two summers, her name disappearing from the register when she was sold to Russia, late in 1896.

"Jupiter"

The "Jupiter" for the South-Western Co. came from Clydebank, and the "Talisman" for the North British from Inglis in 1896. The former is a rather larger and more powerful steamer than the "Neptune" or "Mercury," and forward she is covered in like the "Glen Sannox." Both comfortable and fast, she has all along been a favourite on the Rothesay section. Re-conditioned after the Armistice, she resumed her sailings in 1920, and seems as popular as ever.

"Talisman"

The "Talisman" was of similar dimensions and design of hull and engines to the "Redgauntlet," and was placed on the Rothesay route as a consort to that steamer, taking the place of the "Jeanie Deans." She proved herself a very smart boat; indeed, the North British steamers, although fitted with an older type of machinery than those of the other companies, were never deficient in speed. In re-conditioning after war service, the "Talisman" underwent some improvements, her fore-saloon being extended to the full width of the vessel, and her bridge transferred to forward of the funnel.

"Strathmore"

Captain John Williamson, after disposing of the "Glenmore," laid down with the same builders two steamers of similar design but rather larger, which were to be named "Strathmore" and "Kylemore." The

"Jupiter"

Photo. by the Author

former duly took her place in his fleet, and traded for a time on the Campbeltown route, in succession to the " Culzean Castle." After running for about eleven years, she was bought by the British Government, and now plies on the Solent as the " Harlequin."

" Kylemore "

The second steamer was bought by an English firm while building, and received the name of " Britannia." In 1904 she was brought back, and joining the South-Western fleet as the " Vulcan," was employed on the Fairlie-Millport station, but when the " Strathmore " left the Clyde, this vessel took her place in the Williamson fleet, and was re-christened " Kylemore," the name she was originally intended to bear. She sailed for a season to Inveraray during the war, but was afterwards requisitioned. She now wears her bridge forward of the funnel, an improvement made when she was being re-conditioned.

" Juno "

Clydebank again had the building of a South-Western boat in 1898, the " Juno," on the same general lines as the " Jupiter," but considerably larger and altogether a more massive, weatherly boat. This is the only one of the Clyde boats, so far, constructed with joggled plates. Her engines are powerful and she travels fast. Most of her work has been in the form of excursion-running out of Ayr, and her qualities suit her well for these comparatively exposed waters. After a successful career as a mine-sweeper, she was re-conditioned in

1919, and in the following year was a great acquisition to the depleted fleet on the Firth.

"KENILWORTH"

The "Kenilworth," constructed by Messrs Inglis for the North British Co. in the same year, was a sister-ship to the "Talisman" for the Rothesay section of the Craigendoran service, where these two boats traded successfully up till the outbreak of war. After that event, sailings from Craigendoran south of Dunoon were entirely suspended, and the boats requisitioned. On the "Kenilworth's" return, she underwent similar alterations to those carried out on the "Talisman."

"WAVERLEY" No. 3

The North British boats constructed up to this period were all engined on the non-compound principle, but in the year following the appearance of the "Kenilworth," the company got their first compound-engined steamer, the "Waverley." Again it was Messrs Inglis who got the contract for hull and machinery. The steamer was much larger than anything that had yet appeared at Craigendoran, and had much greater saloon accommodation. Her engines were very powerful, and she attained a speed of over nineteen knots on trial. Her races with the "Jupiter" about the close of last and beginning of the present century recalled some of the earlier days of Clyde steamboating, although by that time the system of pier signals had to a great extent checked the excitement attached to these con-

"Waverley" No. 3

Photo, by Messrs. J. Adamson & Son, Rothesay

TO THE COMING OF THE TURBINE 105

tests. The two boats were well matched, and probably the weather conditions were oftenest the deciding factor in the result. In the "Waverley," as built, the saloon and promenade deck extended only a little way forward of the mast, but in re-conditioning she was covered in right to the bow, in the same way as the "Jupiter," and her bridge was placed forward of the funnel. The alterations seem to have affected her trim, and certainly a speed of nineteen knots is now far beyond her powers.

"King Edward"

Photo. by the Author

CHAPTER X

THE PRESENT CENTURY

THERE were no additions to the fleet in 1900, but the first year of the new century produced a very notable vessel.

"KING EDWARD"

This was the "King Edward," the first of the turbines. This type of engine, the invention of the Hon. C. A. Parsons, was first fitted into the small experimental boat, "Turbinia," in 1894, which is said to have attained the remarkable speed of thirty-four knots, but the system had not been applied to any passenger steamer until the "King Edward" appeared. Nothing like the speed of the "Turbinia" was attempted: such would have been economically impossible in a commercial vessel, but the modest twenty and a half knots of the "King Edward" sufficed to place her well in front of any of the paddle-boats. In dimensions she was identical with the "Duchess of Hamilton," but her two funnels and the absence of paddle-boxes and sponsons gave her quite a different appearance. Of her three shafts, each of the outer two carried originally two propellers, but she was afterwards altered and now has only a single propeller on each shaft. In her internal fittings she is fully equal to the best of the paddle-boats. The "King

Edward" was placed on the Campbeltown station in connection with the South-Western and Caledonian Railways; the public hastened to make trial of the novelty, and their patronage was maintained throughout the season in a manner which showed that her speed and the smoothness of her motion, with its almost entire absence of vibration, were fully appreciated. So encouraging were the results of the first season that her owners decided to lay down a second steamer with Denny, and to cater for the Inveraray trade as well. Placed on this latter route, in opposition to the "Lord of the Isles," the "King Edward" succeeded so well that, within a few years, the old boat was compelled to retire from the contest. During the war the turbines, in common with the paddle-steamers, were requisitioned by Government, but for a different purpose; they were used for transporting troops across the Channel, a duty which they performed with great success. At the close of the war the "King Edward" was acting as an ambulance transport at a port of Northern Europe. She had a very stormy passage home, narrowly escaping shipwreck, but found her way at length to Oban. The last two seasons have found her restored to her original Campbeltown run.

"QUEEN ALEXANDRA" No. 1

The second turbine steamer, the "Queen Alexandra," was about twenty feet longer and fully a knot faster than the "King Edward," and had an upper deck above the promenade deck, reaching from the bridge to a little way abaft of the after funnel. This airy situation was

"Queen Alexandra" No. 1

Photo. by Mr. G. Lithgow, Glasgow

THE PRESENT CENTURY 109

so much enjoyed by passengers, that the owners had the "King Edward" fitted in similar fashion. The new boat took up the Campbeltown sailings, and maintained them until September 1911, when a destructive fire occurred on board her at Greenock. Although sent to her builders and overhauled, this "Queen Alexandra" never reappeared on the Clyde, being sold to the Canadian Pacific Railway Co. for service at Vancouver. Her passage out to that port is said to have been the fastest on record, and she is still running there as the "Princess Patricia."

"Mars"

Messrs John Brown & Co., Ltd., who had now taken over the Clydebank yard, launched two steamers for the railway services in 1902. The "Mars" for the South-Western Co. was of much the same size as the "Minerva" and "Glen Rosa," but forward she was completely covered in like the "Jupiter." This boat took the place of the "Chancellor" on the loch traffic. She has not reappeared on the Clyde since the war, and it has been currently reported that her career was cut short by a mine while sweeping, but the fact that her name still appears in Lloyd's Register would seem to negative this.

"Duchess of Montrose"

The "Duchess of Montrose," for the Caledonian Co., was a smaller edition of the "Duchess of Rothesay," but in her another trial was given to the triple-expansion engine. A useful, though never an outstanding boat, she did service on both Gourock and Wemyss Bay routes until the war, during which she was destroyed by a mine off the French coast. Twelve lives were lost on that occasion.

"Duchess of Fife"

The engine of the "Duchess of Montrose" would seem to have given satisfaction, for another of the same type was fitted into her sister-ship, the "Duchess of Fife," which appeared in the following year. This is the only boat ever built by the Fairfield Co. for the river-service, and she has proved herself a credit to her builders. Designed for only a moderate speed, she far exceeded expectations, and her staunchness suits her well for winter work, in which she is largely employed. More fortunate than her sister-ship, she survived to return to the Clyde after the Armistice.

"Cygnet"

After 1903 there was a complete cessation of building, no new boats being produced for the next three years, if we except the little screw-steamer "Cygnet," added to the MacBrayne fleet in 1904, more for the cargo than the passenger trade. During the coal-strike of 1921, however, her passenger accommodation proved itself very useful, as she was the only steamer plying from the Broomielaw to the coast ports. In the summer of 1906 the "Cygnet" suffered a similar mishap to that which afterwards befell the "Duchess of Rothesay," an open

"Duchess of Argyll"

Photo. by the Author

sea-cock causing her to fill and sink at the Broomielaw. Last summer she did not put in an appearance on the Clyde, having been transferred to one of the Hebridean routes.

"Duchess of Argyll"

In 1906 each of the three railway companies got a new boat. The "Duchess of Argyll" was the first turbine steamer ordered by the Caledonian Co., and she took the place of the "Duchess of Hamilton" on the Ardrossan-Arran station. In dimensions she was identical with that steamer, but her speed was much greater, attaining twenty-two knots on trial, which would appear to stamp her as the fastest of all the Clyde river-boats. When she returned, after serving with success as a transport during the war, an arrangement had already been come to whereby the steamboat traffic between Ardrossan and Arran was to be carried on entirely by the South-Western boats. The old "Ivanhoe" route from Gourock to Arran, by the Kyles, returning by Garroch Head, was thereupon revived, and the "Duchess of Argyll" placed on it with marked success. Advantage was taken of the re-conditioning of this steamer to make an alteration in her design, her open sides, forward of the saloon, being plated, as in the South-Western boats.

"Atalanta"

The South-Western Co. also got their first turbine steamer, the "Atalanta," in the same year. Brown of Clydebank were the builders, and the engines are said to have been an experimental set, constructed as models for the turbines of the "Lusitania," then building at Clydebank. The "Atalanta" was built alongside of that leviathan, and looked very tiny by comparison, although when one goes on board, she is found to be quite a commodious boat. She is, however, neither so large nor so fast as the other turbine steamers on the Firth. Her owners evidently find her a useful boat, for they employ her on different routes as required. Like nearly all her contemporaries, she has war service to her credit.

"Marmion"

The "Marmion," built by Inglis for the North British Co., is a compound-engined paddle-boat, smaller than the "Waverley" and much less powerful, but beautifully fitted. For a number of years she maintained the Arrochar sailings from Craigendoran, in connection with the Loch Long and Loch Lomond circular tour. Minesweeping during the war, she was altered on her return, in similar fashion to the "Waverley," but evidently has not been found satisfactory, as after a single season in commission in the summer of 1920, she has been lying unemployed in Bowling harbour.

"Eagle III."

After three unproductive years, the "Eagle III." was launched for the Buchanan fleet. The hull was built, though not designed, by Messrs Napier & Miller, at Old Kilpatrick; the engine, a single-crank, non-compound diagonal, by Messrs A. & J. Inglis.

"Atalanta"

Photo. by the Author

"Eagle III"

Photo. by Mr. R. D. Orr, Glasgow

THE PRESENT CENTURY 113

Unfortunately, this boat proved deficient in stability, so that it was shortly found necessary to withdraw her in order to have alterations made on her underbody, and she did not resume running until the spring of 1911. The alterations produced the desired effect, the cure being so complete that the steamer not only ran successfully in the passenger trade, but took part in minesweeping operations in the North Sea in war-time. She has been restored to the eleven o'clock run from the Broomielaw to Rothesay, with its supplementary excursions to Loch Striven and round Cumbrae, and the popularity of these with the public proves conclusively that the shortcomings of her early days have not been remembered against her.

"Mountaineer" No. 3

It was also in 1910 that the "Mountaineer" was added to the MacBrayne fleet. She is a short boat with compound diagonal engines and very small paddle-wheels, the tops of the paddle-boxes being flush with the hurricane-deck. The rail round that deck, instead of being open as in the regular Clyde boats, is strongly boarded up, as a protection against the weather likely to be experienced in the Hebridean trade, for which she is primarily intended. Once or twice, however, she has been employed in the winter service between Greenock and the lochs.

"Queen Alexandra" No. 2

1911 brought no new boats, but the sale of the "Queen Alexandra" to the Canadian Pacific Railway Co. about the end of that year led to the laying down of a steamer to replace her. The new boat was of the same dimensions as the old, and the differences in design were of the slightest. She was launched by Denny and took her place on the Campbeltown station in 1912, and has proved quite as popular as her predecessor. Requisitioned for transport work during the war, she transported nearly half a million troops across the Channel, and covered herself with glory by ramming and sinking a German submarine. A brass plate on board bears an inscription recording the exploit, for which her skipper, Captain Angus Keith, received the O.B.E. and the Distinguished Service Cross.

For the past two seasons the "Queen Alexandra" has been transferred to the Inveraray route, the "King Edward" resuming her original station in the Campbeltown trade.

"QUEEN EMPRESS"

In 1912, also, Messrs Murdoch & Murray launched the "Queen Empress," an enlarged and more powerful "Kylemore," for Captain John Williamson. In Government service she figured in various capacities, as troop transport, afterwards as mine-sweeper, and finally as an ambulance transport in the White Sea. In this last occupation she nearly came to grief, and it had been decided to blow her up as she lay aground, to prevent her from falling into the hands of the Bolsheviks, but luckily she floated just in the nick of time and steamed out of danger. Since her return she has been largely employed in excursions from the coast ports.

"Queen Alexandra" No. 2

Photo, by the Author

"Queen Empress"

Photo, by the Author

THE PRESENT CENTURY 115

"FAIR MAID"

No additions have been made to the Clyde fleet for the last ten years, although the North British Co. had an improved "Waverley" laid down with Messrs Inglis in 1914. The "Fair Maid," as she was called, never took her place on the Firth, however, being immediately requisitioned for war-work, and becoming the victim of a German mine.

At the opening of 1912 season, the passenger steamers in commission were: MacBrayne's "Columba" and "Iona"; the Caledonian Co's. "Duchess of Argyll," "Duchess of Hamilton," "Duchess of Rothesay," "Duchess of Fife," "Duchess of Montrose," "Marchioness of Lorne," "Marchioness of Breadalbane" and "Caledonia"; the South-Western Co.'s "Glen Sannox," "Juno," "Atalanta," "Jupiter," "Neptune," "Mercury," "Mars," "Minerva" and "Glen Rosa"; the North British Co.'s "Waverley," "Marmion," "Kenilworth," "Talisman," "Dandie Dinmont" and "Lucy Ashton"; M. T. Clark's "Lord of the Isles" and "Edinburgh Castle"; the Turbine steamers, "Queen Alexandra" and "King Edward"; Williamson's "Queen Empress," "Kylemore" and "Benmore"; Buchanan's "Eagle III.," "Isle of Arran," "Isle of Bute," "Isle of Cumbrae" and "Isle of Skye"; Cameron's "Lady Rowena"; the Firth of Clyde Co.'s "Ivanhoe," and the Campbeltown Co.'s "Davaar" and "Kinloch"; a total of forty-one in all. I omit the "Minard Castle," which had become purely a cargo boat, and also the "Grenadier" and

"Chevalier," which seldom appeared during the summer season.

The season was only a few weeks old when the "Isle of Bute" left the Firth, and at the end of the following year the "Edinburgh Castle" went to the shipbreakers, leaving thirty-nine steamers at the outbreak of war. Of these, twenty-nine were requisitioned by Government, and the maintenance of the Firth service devolved on the remaining ten, with the assistance of the returned "Glen Sannox" and two or three of MacBrayne's old West Highland tourist steamers.

The construction of the boom from Dunoon to the Cloch entailed the dividing of this small fleet into two portions, to work respectively above and below it. On the upper Firth, above the boom, were stationed the two North British boats "Dandie Dinmont" and "Lucy Ashton"; the "Ivanhoe," "Chevalier," "Isle of Cumbrae" and "Lord of the Isles" maintaining the Prince's Pier and Gourock connections. The last-named steamer plied to the Broomielaw until the river was closed to passenger boats. Below the boom, the Rothesay and Millport connections were made from Wemyss Bay by MacBrayne's "Fusilier" and Williamson's "Benmore." The "Columba" was on the Ardrishaig run from Wemyss Bay during part of the war period, permitting the "Iona" to assist the Rothesay service. The Ardrossan-Arran traffic went by the "Glen Sannox" in summer, and in winter by MacBrayne's "Gael" or "Glencoe." The "Davaar" and "Kinloch" were retained in the Campbeltown trade.

The twenty-nine boats taken for war-work were, on

THE PRESENT CENTURY

the whole, fairly fortunate, not more than four, the "Duchess of Hamilton," "Duchess of Montrose," "Neptune" and perhaps the "Mars," being actually lost. Of the others, the "Minerva" was retained by Government, the "Lady Rowena" went to other waters, the "Marchioness of Lorne" has not been re-conditioned, and the "Marmion," after a single season, was laid up, as already stated. The remaining twenty-one resumed their ordinary work on the Firth, and as they came out re-conditioned, a number of the boats that had been plying in war-time gradually disappeared. The "Chevalier," "Fusilier," "Gael" and "Glencoe" went back to their Hebridean services, and the "Ivanhoe," "Isle of Cumbrae," and "Benmore" were withdrawn permanently.

There are thus left twenty-eight steamers, all of which were at work during the past summer of 1922. Two of them belong to Messrs MacBrayne, five to the Caledonian Steam Packet Co., six to the Glasgow and South-Western Railway Co., five to the North British, eight to the combined Williamson, Buchanan and Turbine fleets, and two to the Campbeltown Co.

CHAPTER XI

GENERAL REMARKS

THE different owners' boats are distinguished by their colours, the funnel being the principal mark. Thus, the MacBrayne steamers carry the red funnel with black top, and have the paddle-boxes black with fan-shaped vents. The steamers of the Caledonian Co. have navy-yellow funnels and white paddle-boxes, those of the South-Western Railway Co., red funnels, with black tops, the hull painted grey, and the paddle-boxes white. The North British funnel is red, with white band and black top, paddle-boxes black. The Williamson, Buchanan and Turbine steamers, except the " Lord of the Isles," have white funnels, with black tops. In the exception, the funnels are red, with two white bands divided by a black one, and black top. The paddle-boxes of the " Lord of the Isles " and " Isle of Skye " are black, those of the others white. The Campbeltown boats have the upper portion of the funnel red, and the lower black, with black top. Prior to the Williamson-Buchanan amalgamation, which took place just after the Armistice, the steamers of the Buchanan fleet had black funnels with white bands. This colouring was also borne by Captain Williamson's (senr.) steamers, and by those of Captain John Williamson up to 1897. It was also the funnel of Captain Stewart's boats, which, however, had white paddle-boxes, to distinguish them from the Buchanan and Williamson steamers.

There was a much bigger variety of funnel colourings fifty years ago, when private ownership was the rule, and instead of half a dozen big firms, there were something like a score of different owners running steamers on the Firth. The Hamilton trustees' boats on the Ardrossan-Arran run, the Graham, Brymner boats, and the "Hero" when I first recollect her, had the funnels all-black; the Ayr funnel was cream-coloured; Bob Campbell's Kilmun boats had all-white; Campbell & Gillies' white with black top; the Lochgoil Co.'s the present "Lord of the Isles" funnel. M'Lean's funnel was red with black top and a narrow black hoop half-way up; Shearer's "Glen Rosa" had black with two white bands; the "Chancellor" on the Arrochar run sported the old North British colours, red funnel with black top, and white paddle-boxes; Keith's boats had red funnels with white hoops. Henry Sharp's funnel was red with black top, but this was afterwards altered to black with white band. Hill's Fairlie and Millport steamers had red with black top. The funnels of the "Herald" were cream-coloured, that of the "Culzean Castle" buff with black top, and afterwards red with black top. The "Ivanhoe's" original colours were similar to those of the Caledonian boats, but the paddle-boxes were black. The "Jeanie Deans," when she reappeared on the Clyde as the "Duchess of York," had a funnel like the Lochgoil boats, but with the dividing band red instead of black; in the following year the hull and paddle-boxes were painted grey, the funnel buff with two red bands and a white one between,

GENERAL REMARKS

with buff top. As already mentioned, the "Guinevere" had frequent changes when on the Arran route. These included all-black, red with black top, buff with black top, black with white hoops and red with white hoops. On the Rothesay run she carried the Buchanan black with white band. In Cameron's hands, the "Madge Wildfire" bore the Caledonian colours, but with black-topped funnel; but the "Lady Rowena," during her first season for him, had red funnel with black top and dark green hull and paddle-boxes. She was afterwards painted to match the "Madge." "Ivanhoe," when she went into the up-river trade, was given white funnels with very narrow black tops.

A number of the owners had their own designs of paddle-boxes, apart from colouring, but in the case of bought-in boats they seldom went to the expense of altering them, at least until renewals were required. Messrs MacBrayne alone made it their practice to fit all their purchases with their own design with the fan-shaped vents. Among steamers that had the paddle-box design altered are the "Hero," "Sultan," "Cumbrae," "Eagle," "Argyle," "Elaine," "Lancelot," "Guinevere," "Edinburgh Castle," "Isle of Cumbrae" and "Chancellor" No. 3. The "Sheila," on the other hand, notwithstanding two changes of ownership and name, retained the old Wemyss Bay design of paddle-box all the thirty-five years she sailed on the Clyde.

A very striking and pleasing feature of the Clyde service during all these fifty years has been its almost complete immunity from serious accident. I cannot recall a single instance of a passenger having lost his life as the result of a mishap to any of the steamboats; the drowning of the " Kintyre's " engineer when she was sunk is the only fatality I can call to mind. When we think of the great number of passengers conveyed every morning during the season from all the coast ports to the different railway termini, the routes crossing one another, and every steamer pressed to her utmost to make her railway connection in time, we cannot fail to admire the skill that has been exercised in navigating these narrow and busy waters, and the precautions that must have been taken to ensure the perfect condition of engines and steering-gear, whose sudden failure at a critical moment might readily have brought about serious disaster. Mishaps to the boats there have been, by stranding, collision and fire, some of which are recorded in the foregoing pages. In one or two instances, these happenings have been alarming enough, as when " Columba " and " Sheila," racing for Innellan pier, collided, and the latter had to be beached to prevent sinking; but only three boats, " Kintyre," " Lady Gertrude " and " Vesta," have been totally lost in their native waters.

The increase of railway facilities, coupled with the deplorably filthy state of the river in the seventies and eighties, brought about a great reduction in the traffic from the Broomielaw, passengers preferring to embark at Prince's Pier, Gourock, Craigendoran or Wemyss Bay rather than face the alternative of sailing down the evil-smelling stream. Of late years, since the purification scheme has alleviated the discomforts of the river journey, there has been a marked revival in the Broomielaw trade, the delightful excursions and

GENERAL REMARKS

remarkably low fares offered by Messrs Buchanan's steamers having proved very attractive to the day-tripper. But, with it all, even in the height of the season, not more than half a dozen steamers leave the Bridge Wharf in a day, whereas, fifty years ago the average was sixteen or seventeen.

A number of years ago Messrs Buchanan commenced a Sunday service. By that time, however, the conditions were vastly different from those that prevailed in the old days of " Petrel " and " Kingstown." The Act which prohibited the sale of liquor on Sundays on board steamers returning to port the same evening had deprived Sunday sailing of the only attraction it possessed for the class that patronised these boats, and the absence of such undesirables made it possible for a respectable class of passengers to enjoy Sunday on the Firth under decorous conditions. For some years prior to the war the Caledonian Co. ran a steamer from Gourock to Dunoon and Rothesay on Sunday forenoons, returning in the evening, but although always well patronised, the service has not been resumed since the Armistice.

The constantly growing demand for greater luxury in travel has brought about a continuous improvement in the comfort of the boats, until at length the old flush-deckers and raised-quarterdeck boats have entirely disappeared, and we have a fleet composed entirely of steamers equipped with luxuriously furnished deck saloons, well lighted and ventilated. Dainty tea-rooms and well-furnished sweet and book stalls, formerly undreamt of, are now regarded as essential parts of a steamer's outfit.

No felt-hatted skipper now mounts the paddle-box to ply the knocker; instead, a gold-braided dignitary paces the commodious bridge, and manipulates the telegraph, crossing from side to side as occasion demands without the inconvenience of making his way among the passengers. He is free to devote his attention fully to the navigation of the ship, for a brass-bound purser relieves him from the duty of collecting the fares, with its accompanying clerical work. On the bridge, too, is found space for the steersman, whose task is lightened by the substitution of steam-steering gear for the heavy and intractable hand-wheel.

The fiddler or harpist who found a place abaft the engine-house, and drew a haphazard remuneration from the caprice of the passengers, has given way to a uniformed band, whose collections are made on a business-like system.

In the engine-rooms, presided over by uniformed chiefs, the old single-expansion engine is yet far from obsolete, despite the introduction of compound, triple-expansion and turbine machinery. Of the boats plying last season, six are screw steamers, four of them with three-shaft turbines, and two single-screws with reciprocating engines of compound inverted type; of the twenty-two paddle-boats, ten are fitted with compound two-crank diagonals, three with compound tandem diagonals with single crank, one with triple tandem diagonal, three with single-expansion oscillators, and five with the single-cylinder diagonal, so much in vogue in the seventies.

Perhaps the period that witnessed the greatest improvement in the boats was the earlier half of the nineties, when the Caledonian and South-Western Companies were strenuously competing to secure the trade for their Gourock and Prince's Pier routes respectively, and vied with each other in equipping their steamers with everything that could prove attractive to the passenger. The policy of "live and let live" which succeeded this rivalry has, no doubt, proved more profitable to the companies, but has not tended to improve the service from the passenger's point of view. It is astonishing to find, with all the improvements in machinery, that the speed of the boats shows little if any advance in the last half-century. Of course, it would not be reasonable to expect record passages from the Broomielaw, such as were made in the early sixties, when the all-the-way steamers were competing with the Greenock Railway. There is no longer a call for fast boats on the river route, as it can never again be a serious competitor of the railways, and in any case the reckless disregard of river regulations which went to the making of these fast runs would not be tolerated nowadays, so that the passage of two hours, twenty-eight minutes from Glasgow to Rothesay, accomplished by Simons's "Rothesay Castle" in 1861, is not likely ever to be excelled. But even on the open Firth, it is at least doubtful if we have a paddle-boat to-day that could "run the lights" from Cloch to Cumbrae in forty-five minutes, a feat performed by the second "Iona" nearly sixty years ago, and you will search last season's time-tables in vain for a railway connection to Rothesay equalling in speed the 4.35 express placed on the Wemyss Bay route forty-five years ago, whose passengers were regularly landed on

Rothesay quay at five minutes from six, eighty minutes from Bridge Street.

The fact is that the Clyde, whose river-steamers were once unrivalled, has of late years allowed its fleet to get behind the times. Of the fifteen steamers plying for the three railway companies during the past summer, only three were built during the present century, and although irreproachable upkeep has ensured that the standard of comfort is fully maintained, the speed of the boats has deteriorated, and their war experiences have not tended to make them faster. While one can admire the sentiment that keeps such veterans as "Glencoe" running on tourist routes, where speed is not essential, it is but reasonable to expect that railway connections on the Firth should be maintained by fast boats. Even the original twenty-two knots of the "Duchess of Argyll" is but a moderate gait as speeds are reckoned nowadays. I cannot help hoping that the drop in shipbuilding costs will induce the companies to lay down some really fast boats, fast according to modern ideas, that will regain for the Clyde Firth service the proud position it formerly held.

APPENDICES

"Clutha" No. 6

Photo. lent by Mr. James Wotherspoon, Glasgow

APPENDIX I

THE "CLUTHAS"

In April 1884 the Clyde Trustees, who had obtained powers under the Clyde Navigation Act of 1878, to run steamers, inaugurated a passenger service within the limits of the harbour.

On the 12th of that month four small steamers started running between Victoria Bridge and Whiteinch, a distance of about $4\frac{1}{2}$ miles, with calls at Glasgow Bridge, Springfield Lane, Finnieston, Highland Lane (Govan), Meadowside, Sawmill Road and Linthouse.

The boats, which all bore the name of "Clutha," and were numbered 1, 2, 3 and 4, were built by Messrs Seath of Rutherglen. They were twin-screws, with engines of non-compound type placed amidships, and small cabins forward and abaft of the engine-house. They measured 74 feet by 13 feet, and had accommodation for 235 passengers. Forward of the funnel was a low erection serving as a bridge, the steering being done by the skipper. The boats had no masts, the "masthead" light being carried on a long stanchion, forked at the upper end. At the various places of call were floating landing-stages, at a constant level with the steamer's decks. The fare was a penny for any distance, and the service, linking up as it did the two sides of the river, enjoyed such popularity that two larger boats were added to the fleet in the same year. "Cluthas" 5 and 6 were by the same builders as the original boats, but much larger, measuring 102 feet by 14 feet, and carrying 350 passengers. Their machinery was of the same description as in the first four boats, but more powerful. Nothing further was added till 1890, when "Cluthas" 7 and 8 came from Messrs Murray's yard at Dumbarton, with compound engines by Messrs M. Paul & Co. These were short steamers, of greater beam than their predecessors, their dimensions being 80 feet by 16 feet, and their passenger capacity 315. In the following year the same builders produced two larger steamers, Nos. 9 and 10, 90 feet by 17 feet, and certificated for 360 passengers. This pair also had compound engines by Messrs Paul. After another interval of five years, Nos. 11 and 12 appeared. They were of the same dimensions as Nos. 9 and 10, but carried only 331 passengers; their builders were Messrs Russell & Co., Port-Glasgow, and their compound engines were by Messrs Muir & Houston. No further steamers were built, as the service, which had up to this time been a profitable one, began now to suffer from the competition of other enterprises. The District Subway, opened in January 1897, diverted part of the traffic from the "Cluthas," and the electric trams, introduced by the Glasgow Corporation in 1901, proved disastrous to them. The steamboats ceased to be remunerative, and a reduction in the number of sailings leading to no improvement, the undertaking was abandoned at the end of November 1903. The last run was made by "Clutha" No. 11 on the 30th of that month, the master being William Sinclair, the oldest skipper of the fleet; the engineer, James Thomson; the collector of fares, John M'Millan; and the rope-boy, Albert Henderson.

Of the steamers, which were all twin-screws, of 9 to 10 knots speed, two—Nos. 1 and 4—were retained by the Clyde Trustees, the former being used as a messenger boat, the latter fitted up as a yacht and re-named "Comet." No. 2 was bought by Messrs Denny of Dumbarton, and No. 3 by a firm of stevedores at Grangemouth, while No. 5 went to London owners. No. 6 was bought by a Mr Wilson of Bo'ness, and saw some war service on the Forth. In February 1918 she became the property of a Mr M'Gillivray of Macduff. Nos. 7 and 8 were sold to Messrs Hawthorn, Leslie & Co., of Hebburn-on-Tyne, and Nos. 9 and 10 to the Admiralty. No. 11 went into the hands of the Mayor and Aldermen of Bangor, Wales. She

APPENDIX I

was in war service at Preston, and in 1920 was purchased by the Borough of Middlesbrough, and re-named "Lady Magdalene." No. 12 went to Ireland, plying on Lough Neagh as the "Lough Neagh Queen" for a Mr M'Ghee of Toome Bridge. Afterwards she was on Loch Leven as the "Loch Leven Queen," becoming later the property of Messrs MacBrayne, who again re-named her "Lochness," and placed her on the Inverness and Fort-Augustus station.

It is pleasant to record that the "Cluthas" enjoyed the same immunity from serious accident as the regular Clyde fleet, not a single fatality occurring in the whole period of twenty years, during which this interesting and well-nigh forgotten enterprise was carried on. This seems little short of miraculous, in view of the fact that when the traffic was at its zenith the steamers were carrying over two and a half millions of passengers annually.

APPENDIX II

LIST OF PASSENGER STEAMERS IN THE CLYDE FIRTH TRADE SINCE 1872

i.p.=iron paddle. i.s.=iron single screw. i. & s.p.=iron and steel pad. s.p.=steel paddle. s.s.=steel single screw. s.tr.s.=steel triple-screw. w.p.=wooden paddle.

Name.	Description.	Built.	Dimensions.
Adela	i.p.	1877	207' × 19' 2" × 7' 4"
Ardencaple	i.p.	1866	150' × 16' 2" × 6' 2"
Ardgowan	i.p.	1866	150' × 16' 2" × 6' 2"
Ardmore (ex-Sultan).			
Arran (ex-Dunoon Castle).			
Argyle	i.p.	1866	177' × 17' 5" × 7' 6"
Argyll	s.s.	1885	140' × 23' × 9'
Atalanta	s.tr.s.	1906	210' × 30' 1" × 10' 3"
Athole	i.p.	1866	192' × 18' 5" × 7' 8"
Balmoral	i.p.	1842	136' × 18' 2" × 7' 9"
Benmore	i.p.	1876	201' × 19' 1" × 7' 3"
Bonnie Doon (1)	i.p.	1870	202' × 19' 2" × 7' 6"
Bonnie Doon (2)	i.p.	1876	218' × 20' × 7' 5"
Brigadier (ex-Cygnus).			
Brodick Castle	i.p.	1878	207' × 21' 7" × 7' 5"
Caledonia	s.p.	1889	200' × 22' × 7' 5"
Carrick Castle	i.p.	1870	192' × 18' × 7' 4"
Carrick Castle (2) (ex-Culzean Castle).			
Chancellor (2)	i.p.	1864	163' × 18' 7" × 7'
Chancellor (3)	s.p.	1880	199' × 21' 1" × 8' 2"
Chevalier	i.p.	1866	211' × 22' 2" × 9' 3"
Columba	s.p.	1878	301' × 27' 1" × 9' 4"
Craigrownie	i.p.	1870	175' × 17' 1" × 6' 8"
Culzean Castle	s.p.	1891	246' × 27' 6" × 10' 2"

APPENDIX II

Name.	Description.	Built.	Dimensions.
Cumbrae (ex-Marquis of Lorne).			
Cygnet	s.s.	1904	135' × 21' 1" × 9' 4"
Cygnus	i.p.	1854	182' × 21' 4" × 9' 7"
Dandie Dinmont (1)	i.p.	1866	197' × 22' 1" × 6' 9"
Dandie Dinmont (2)[1]	s.p.	1895	195' × 22' 1" × 7' 2"
Daniel Adamson (ex-Chancellor 2).			
Davaar	s.s.	1885	217' × 27' × 12' 9"
Diana Vernon	i. & s.p.	1885	180' × 18' 1" × 7' 1"
Duchess of Argyll	s.tr.s.	1906	250' × 30' 1" × 10' 1"
Duchess of Fife	s.p.	1903	210' × 25' × 8' 5"
Duchess of Hamilton	s.p.	1890	250' × 30' 1" × 10'
Duchess of Montrose	s.p.	1902	210' × 25' 1" × 8' 7"
Duchess of Rothesay	s.p.	1895	225' × 26' 1" × 8' 6"
Duchess of York (ex-Jeanie Deans).			
Dunoon Castle	i.p.	1867	191' × 18' 2" × 7' 5"
Eagle	i.p.	1864	219' × 20' 5" × 7' 3"
Eagle III.	s.p.	1910	215' × 25' 1" × 8' 1"
Edinburgh Castle	i.p.	1879	205' × 19' 9" × 7' 6"
Elaine	i.p.	1867	175' × 17' 1" × 6' 6"
Fusilier	s.p.	1888	202' × 21' 6" × 8' 1"
Gael	i.p.	1867	211' × 23' 2" × 10' 6"
Galatea	s.p.	1889	230' × 25' 1" × 7' 8"
Gareloch	i.p.	1872	180' × 18' 2" × 6' 8"
Glencoe (ex-Mary Jane).			
Glenmore	s.p.	1895	190' × 21' 7" × 7' 2"
Glen Rosa (1)	i.p.	1877	206' × 20' 1" × 7' 5"
Glen Rosa (2)	s.p.	1893	200' × 25' × 8' 3"
Glen Sannox	s.p.	1892	260' × 30' 1" × 10' 1"
Grenadier	s.p.	1885	222' × 23' 1" × 9' 3"
Guinevere	i.p.	1869	200' × 19' 1" × 6' 8"
Guy Mannering (ex-Sheila).			
Heather Bell	i.p.	1871	207' × 21' × 8' 8"
Herald	i.p.	1866	221' × 22' × 10' 4"
Hero	i.p.	1858	181' × 19' 1" × 7' 1"
Industry	w.p.	1814	66' × 14' 7" × 8' 1"
Inveraray Castle	i.p.	1839	172' × 20' 5" × 9' 3"
Iona	i.p.	1864	255' × 25' 6" × 9'

[1] Afterwards lengthened to 209'.

CLYDE RIVER-STEAMERS

Name.	Description.	Built.	Dimensions.
Isle of Arran	s.p.	1892	210' × 24' 1" × 7' 4"
Isle of Bute (ex-Sheila).			
Isle of Cumbrae (ex-Jeanie Deans).			
Isle of Skye (ex-Madge Wildfire).			
Ivanhoe	i.p.	1880	225' × 22' 2" × 8' 3"
Jeanie Deans	i. & s.p.	1884	210' × 20' 1" × 7' 6"
Juno	s.p.	1898	245' × 29' 1" × 9' 7"
Jupiter	s.p.	1896	230' × 28' 1" × 9'
Kenilworth	s.p.	1898	215' × 23' 1" × 7' 6"
King Edward	s.tr.s.	1901	250' × 30' 1" × 10'
Kingstown	i.p.	1862	151' × 20' 1" × 7' 3"
Kinloch	i.s.	1878	205' × 24' 1" × 12' 7"
Kintyre	i.s.	1868	184' × 22' 9" × 11' 5"
Kylemore	s.p.	1897	200' × 24' 1" × 7' 7"
Lady Clare	s.p.	1891	180' × 19' 3" × 6' 5"
Lady Gertrude	i.p.	1872	190' × 18' × 7' 6"
Lady of the Isles (ex-Lord of the Isles, 1).			
Lady Rowena	s.p.	1891	200' × 21' 1" × 6' 7"
Lancelot	i.p.	1868	191' × 18' × 6' 9"
Largs	i.p.	1864	161' × 19' 1" × 7' 9"
Levan	i.p.	1866	150' × 16' 2" × 6' 2"
Lord of the Isles (1)	i.p.	1877	246' × 24' 2" × 9'
Lord of the Isles (2)	s.p.	1891	255' × 25' 6" × 9' 1"
Lorne	i.p.	1871	211' × 19' 1" × 7' 4"
Lough Foyle	i.p.	1853	163' × 16' 3" × 7' 1"
Lucy Ashton	s.p.	1888	190' × 21' 7" × 7' 2"
Madge Wildfire	s.p.	1886	190' × 20' × 7' 5"
Marchioness of Breadalbane	s.p.	1890	200' × 22' 1" × 7' 5"
Marchioness of Bute	s.p.	1890	200' × 22' 1" × 7' 5"
Marchioness of Lorne	s.p.	1891	200' × 24' × 8' 3"
Marmion	s.p.	1906	210' × 24' × 8' 3"
Marquis of Bute	i.p.	1868	196' × 18' 1" × 7' 3"
Marquis of Lorne	i.p.	1863	176' × 17' 6" × 6' 8"
Mars	s.p.	1902	200' × 26' 1" × 8' 6"
Mary Jane	i.p.	1846	165' × 20' 2" × 9' 4"
Meg Merrilies	i.p.	1883	210' × 21' 4" × 7' 2"
Mercury	s.p.	1892	220' × 26' × 9' 2"

APPENDIX II

Name.	Description.	Built.	Dimensions.
Minard Castle . .	s.s.	1882	140′ × 22′ × 10′ 4″
Minerva . . .	s.p.	1893	200′ × 25′ × 8′ 3″
Mountaineer (1) .	i.p.	1852	195′ × 18′ 2″ × 8′ 2″
Mountaineer (2) (ex-Hero).			
Mountaineer (3) .	s.p.	1910	180′ × 20′ 1″ × 7′ 7″
Neptune . . .	s.p.	1892	220′ × 26′ × 9′ 2″
Petrel . . .	i.p.	1845	168′ × 18′ × 8′ 4″
Prince of Wales .	i.p.	1845	127′ × 21′ 2″ × 7′ 8″
Queen Alexandra (1)	s.tr.s.	1902	270′ × 32′ 1″ × 11′ 6″
Queen Alexandra (2)	s.tr.s.	1912	270′ × 32′ 1″ × 11′ 1″
Queen Empress .	s.p.	1912	210′ × 25′ 6″ × 8′ 4″
Redgauntlet . .	s.p.	1895	215′ × 22′ 1″ × 7′ 4″
Rothesay Castle .	i.p.	1865	203′ × 19′ 3″ × 7′ 9″
Scotia . . .	i.p.	1880	211′ × 21′ 8″ × 8′ 3″
Seagull . . .	i.p.	1877	121′ × 19′ 4″ × 7′ 7″
Shandon (ex-Chancellor 2).			
Sheila . . .	i.p.	1877	205′ × 20′ × 7′ 7″
Strathmore . .	s.p.	1897	200′ × 24′ 1″ × 7′ 7″
Sultan . . .	i.p.	1861	176′ × 16′ 6″ × 7′ 2″
Sultana . . .	i.p.	1868	188′ × 18′ 3″ × 7′ 5″
Talisman . .	s.p.	1896	215′ × 23′ × 7′ 5″
The Lady Mary .	i.p.	1868	173′ × 20′ × 8′ 3″
Undine . . .	i.p.	1865	200′ × 18′ 5″ × 7′ 7″
Vale of Clwyd . .	i.p.	1865	186′ × 18′ 1″ × 7′
Venus . . .	i.p.	1852	159′ × 17′ 1″ × 8′ 2″
Vesta . . .	i.p.	1853	162′ × 16′ 5″ × 6′ 8″
Viceroy [1] . .	i.p.	1875	194′ × 20′ 1″ × 7′
Victoria . . .	s.p.	1886	222′ × 23′ 1″ × 8′
Vivid . . .	i.p.	1864	197′ × 18′ 2″ × 7′ 8″
Vulcan (1) . .	i.p.	1854	167′ × 16′ 3″ × 8′
Vulcan (2) (see Kylemore).			
Waverley (2) . .	s.p.	1885	205′ × 21′ 1″ × 7′ 5″
Waverley (3) . .	s.p.	1899	235′ × 26′ 1″ × 8′ 4″
Windsor Castle .	i.p.	1875	195′ × 19′ × 7′ 2″

[1] Afterwards lengthened to 208′.